The Complete Book Of
GARDEN ORNAMENTS,
COMPLEMENTS,
AND ACCESSORIES

The Complete Book Of
GARDEN ORNAMENTS, COMPLEMENTS, AND ACCESSORIES

DANIEL J. FOLEY

CROWN PUBLISHERS, Inc., New York

For Allen C. Haskell
and Edward D. Pacheko

© 1972 by Daniel J. Foley
Library of Congress Catalog Card Number: 70–147324
ISBN: 0-517-500787
Inquiries should be addressed to
Crown Publishers, Inc., 419 Park Avenue South, New York, N.Y. 10016.

Printed in the United States of America
Published simultaneously in Canada by
General Publishing Company Limited
Designed by Michael Perpich

Contents

Acknowledgments

THESE pages of acknowledgment are little more than an attempt to express my gratitude for help, advice, and assistance extended in the preparation of this book. The owners and creators of some of the objects illustrated are not known to me while others have chosen to remain anonymous. To each and every one I extend my heartfelt thanks.

To Margaret M. Foley, Arlene R. O'Shea, and Elizabeth S. Hunt for typing the manuscript and various clerical and editorial details.

To the following photographers for illustrations: Douglas Armsden, Stephen T. Cahill, Elizabeth B. Freeman, Paul E. Genereux, Richard Merrill, Paul Picone, Herbert Rea, John P. Roche, Donald Robinson, Ronald Rolo, and especially to George Taloumis for his extensive collection.

To Duane Doolittle and Cobb Blake for reviving the work of Eric Soderholtz.

To Allen C. Haskell and Edward D. Pacheko for sharing their garden know-how in countless ways, and to John R. Burbidge for creating examples of sculptural collage for the enjoyment of gardeners.

To Mr. and Mrs. Moses Alpers for sharing their garden and their enthusiasm for garden ornaments.

To my associates whose names appear on these pages, to members of manufacturing firms, also acknowledged individually, and to owners of gardens and garden ornaments who shared their possessions and allowed them to be photographed, I am most grateful. The list that follows includes them in part.

Peter P. Abate, Mr. and Mrs. Moses Alpers, James F. Baker, James Howland Ballou, Mr. and Mrs. Robert B. M. Barton, Mrs. Robert H. Bishop, Cobb Blake, Cary Bok, Mrs. Richard Bowman, Brookgreen Gardens, Mary C. Bunting, John R. Burbidge, Miss Lee Burnham, Andrew Bye, California Redwood Association, Colonial Williamsburg, Mrs. Marcus E. Cox, Mr. Larry M. Coy III, Roderick W. Cumming, Mr. and Mrs. Raymond L. Cummings, Mrs. Horace E. Davenport, Gerald Davis, Duane Doolittle, Mr. and Mrs. Fred T. Douglas, George Driver, Alden R. Eaton, Robert A. Edwards, Essex Institute, Carl Frasier, Mr. and Mrs. William W. K. Freeman, John Frongelo, Joseph W. P. Frost, Isabella Stewart Gardner Museum, Mrs. Stuart N. Gardner, Edward Garratt, Mr. and Mrs. Carl Goddard, Mrs. Carl Haffenreffer, Mrs. William T. Haley, Mrs. C. A. B. Halvorson, Mr. and Mrs. James R. Hammond, Roland Hammond, Mrs. Montgomery Harkins, Allen C. Haskell, Warren Hassmer, Rebekah Hobbs, Mrs. Calvin Hosmer, Jr., House of the Seven Gables, Mrs. John M. Howells, Mrs. Fitch Ingersoll, Mrs. Nils R. Johaneson, Mrs. Anthony F. Kearney, Lee Kelson, Hartwell Kennard, Mrs. Frederick Kingsbury, Viola B. Kneeland, Langdon Memorial, David B. Little, Mrs. Philip H. Lord, Mrs. Hollis Lovell, Edward J. Luzinski, Kenneth Lynch, Marie Lynch, Louis Mangifesti, R. Newton Mayall, James P. McCarvill, William W. McTyeire III, Frank Miller, Mrs. Alfred S. Moses, The Mount Vernon Ladies' Association, Museum of

Modern Art, Don O'Connor, Charles O'Donnell, Mr. and Mrs. James A. O'Shea, Jr.,
Thomas O'Shea, Edward D. Pacheko, Mrs. Edward P. Parker,
Mr. and Mrs. H. Berkley Peabody, Peabody Museum, Wilfred J. Pelletier, Pennsylvania
Horticultural Society, Robert Perry, Mr. and Mrs. John Pickering, Paul Picone, The Ragged
Sailor (Camden, Maine, and Tiburon, California), Leonard J. Raymond, William Reynard,
Mrs. Robert Richardson, Mrs. Gordon Roaf, Donald Robinson, Edward B. Rushford,
Heine Scotoni, Mrs. Donald C. Seamans, Mrs. Ellery Sedgwick, Leonard V. Short,
Mrs. William H. Shreve, David Sinclair, Mr. and Mrs. C. Fred Smith, Jr., George Warren
Smith, James Sproul, Edward Storey, Gurdon L. Tarbox, Jr., Dr. Irvin Taube,
Donald R. Taylor, Mrs. Irene B. Thompson, Tryon Palace Restoration, Mrs. Jane Abbot Tyler,
Mrs. Abbott Payson Usher, Walpole Woodworkers, Inc., E. G. Washburne & Company,
Mrs. Foster Whitney.

Daniel J. Foley
Salem, Massachusetts

Introduction

Comparatively few books are written single-handedly, and more than half the fun of "doing" a book, particularly one of this sort, is derived from the help extended by friends, art specialists and craftsmen as well as photographers and museum curators, whose sharp eyes, knowledge, and enthusiasm often focus attention on objects and material that might otherwise be overlooked.

This volume is essentially a picture book of garden ornaments and accessories, written to help gardeners find suitable objects for embellishing their grounds. Notes on the history and background of many of the pieces are offered to relate them to their settings and to suggest ways in which using them and other objects of a similar nature may add interest to present-day gardens. The detailed history of garden ornament as it relates to landscape art is to be found in the lengthy list of books in the bibliography.

Gardens in America, large and small, public and private, are surprisingly rich in garden ornament even though a good part of it lays no claim to being American in origin. Since our gardens and public parks have drawn heavily on Europe for inspiration in the matter of design, it is only natural that the ornaments used to embellish them should stem from the same source.

For nearly three centuries, American gardeners and garden designers have been content to rely upon tradition for the choice and use of garden ornament. As a result, sculpture, fountains, containers, and other garden objects of a decorative nature, executed in the contemporary manner, are seen all too seldom except when specially designed to complement a contemporary building or planting, usually of public or institutional use. Comparatively few owners of contemporary houses and grounds have exploited the possibilities of using some of the newer art forms for garden decoration. Obviously, this is a facet of garden art yet to be developed.

To assist gardeners in finding suitable garden ornaments, a directory of sources is included which lists firms that advertise extensively. In addition, many sculptors as well as skilled craftsmen and artisans working in stone, metal, wood, and fabricated materials commercial outlets for their work but are content to execute special commissions for clients. produce notable work that is available only by way of discovery. Few have agents or Often these individuals are prime sources of unique garden ornaments. They are worth seeking.

1

THREE CENTURIES OF GARDEN ORNAMENT

MANY of the earliest dooryard gardens planted along the Atlantic seaboard faced on the ocean or on some inlet from the sea, or had their setting near a river, a stream, a lake, or a pond. Enclosed by fences made of whatever was at hand—wattles, palings, or simple rails—these little plots were filled with herbs, culinary and medicinal, as well as favorite flowers of the Old World. (Vegetables, tree fruits, and berry bushes required more space than the dooryard allowed.) In many ways, these dooryard plantings provided a nostalgic link with cottage gardens left behind across the sea. Simple plots, they boasted of few ornaments except the plants themselves—"the fair white lily and the sweet fragrant rose," and such trees as the "lasting cedar," the "knottie maple," the "pallied birch" and the like, and a few shrubs—sumach, elderberry, seaside roses, or other native kinds—were allowed to stand around each homestead as the land was cleared.

More utilitarian than ornamental were the fences which were built quickly by virtue of necessity and, although purely functional and rustic in appearance, are considered definitely picturesque when reproduced today. Wattle fences were made by driving palings into the ground at measured intervals and weaving grape canes or willow twigs between them to create a basket-weave effect, which is notably decorative when well made. These were built high enough to keep out the sheep, goats, and other animals. Palings fastened to a frame of posts and rails made a crude picket fence. Stockade fences made of palings were considerably higher.

Domelike bee skeps, woven from straw, were a much-needed commodity to supply honey so essential to everyday living. These skeps were handsome ornaments as well, but perhaps not so to the puritan housewife. The few settlers who owned brass sundials were fortunate indeed. Those to be found in the earliest settlements were brought from England. If there was a bench in the garden, chances are it was a log cut in half lengthwise. Ground clamshells, contrasting noticeably in their whiteness with the dark earth, were scattered on the walks t absorb the moisture in the muddy paths, or so it is believed. If a housewife ventured to a knot pattern (a garden planted in a design), it must have been a simple one since th little time for practicing the niceties of the art of gardening at home in England. Bu thing we are certain. As Nathaniel Hawthorne expressed it, "There is not a softe found in the character of those stern men than that they should have been sens flower-roots clinging among the fibres of their rugged hearts, and felt the ne them over sea, and making them hereditary in the new land." For the mo

make
ere was
, of one
trait to be
ble of those
cessity of bringing
st part, the

Elias Hasket Derby's teahouse, designed by Samuel McIntire in 1794, was moved to the garden at Glen Magna in Danvers, Massachusetts, in 1901.

(Opposite)

Among the few remaining early American wooden ornaments made especially for a garden is "Figure of Plenty," now known as "Pomona." She was carved by John and Simeon Skillin of Boston in 1793 as one of a series of wooden sculptures made for the garden and teahouse of Elias Hasket Derby of South Danvers. An impressive young lady she is, attired in the height of late eighteenth century fashion. Her gown hangs in lifelike folds, her hat sits at a jaunty angle on her beautifully coiffed head, her feet are fitted out with pretty little slippers, and she holds a cornucopia overflowing with fruit. This skillfully executed and painted figure is life-size, standing fifty-five inches tall, rather a majestic height for a lady of that era. She originally was placed on a pedestal in front of the teahouse which was designed by Samuel McIntire, the famous Salem architect and carver. "Pomona" now resides in an alcove in the Octagonal Room of the Peabody Museum. *Photo, Richard Merrill. Courtesy, Peabody Museum*

conspicuous ornaments of the early gardens in the New World were essentially those specimens of verdant sculpture, lovingly planted for their beauty and fragrance—the rose, the lily, the hollyhock, the lavender hedge, the box bush, and a host of others.

The brilliant attire in which the maples, oaks, and sassafrases decked themselves in autumn was an experience new to the pioneers—a spectacle more eye-catching than any man-made garden ornament. They had not known such spectacular pageants of fall color at home. True, some trees and shrubs of the English countryside change color as summer wanes, but generally the effects are much more subdued than what they witnessed in the new land. The golden days of October and early November were indeed an inspiration for these homesick settlers, ill equipped to face the rigors of the wilderness, but determined to establish themselves and their way of life. Somehow, they survived and flourished and those "flower-roots clinging among the fibres of their rugged hearts" actually took root in the virgin soil of Colonial America. Thomas Morton, a contemporary of Bradford and Winthrop expressed himself thus: "I did not think that in all the known world it could be parallel'd for so many goodly groves of trees, dainty fine round rising hillucks, delicate faire large plains, sweet crystal fountaines, and cleare running streams that twine in fine meanders through the meads, making so sweet a mumering noise to heare as would even fill the sense with delight a sleepe, so pleasantly doe they glide upon the pebble stones, jetting most jocundly where they doe meete and hand in hand runne downe to Neptune's Court, to pay yearly tribute which they owe him as soveraigne Lord of all springs."

Leaving New England for the warmer climate of Virginia provides us with a poetic glimpse of the garden of William Byrd II. In 1705 Byrd's brother-in-law, Robert Beverley, in an attempt to set English readers straight about conditions in the New World colony, wrote a book entitled *The History and Present State of Virginia*. Since he also hoped to lure professional gardeners, he wrote: "Have you pleasure in a Garden? All things thrive in it, most surprisingly; you can't walk by a Bed of Flowers, but besides the entertainment of their Beauty, your Eyes will be saluted with the charming colors of the Humming Bird, which revels among the Flowers. . . . Colonel Byrd, in his garden which is the finest in that Country, has a Summer-House set round with the Indian Honey-Suckle which all the summer is continually full of sweet Flowers, in which these Birds delight exceedingly." He went on to mention summerhouses, arbors, and grottoes where one could retreat from "the inconvenience of heat."

Gardens grew and flourished in Williamsburg and elsewhere in Virginia. Lady Skipworth wrote enthusiastically about her garden as did others. New plants by the dozen were introduced and, together with native wild flowers and bulbs in the spring, the long growing season had its highlights of color, lasting until late November. More than thirty years ago, the colonial town of Williamsburg was restored to its pristine glory, and improvements and changes are still being made. No group of colonial plantings in America has been more vividly pictured and described so that to attempt a complete word picture in this volume would not be practical. The photographs speak for themselves. Millions of Americans know these gardens and are the richer for it.

The highlights of Mount Vernon as they depict garden ornament are to be found in these pages, along with other notable gardens of historic interest, in an attempt to bring into sharper focus the part that ornament has played in American gardens.

Aside from those of Colonial Williamsburg and Mount Vernon, among the most impressive gardens in America today are those which have been restored at Tryon Palace at New Bern,

The art of carpet bedding, the arrangement of low-growing plants into beds to form a symmetrical pattern or picture, reached its zenith in Victorian England and was widely copied in the United States. Examples can still be seen in public parks and municipal plantings around the world. An amateur gardener, Jim Sproul of Ocean City, New Jersey, has designed and executed a number of carpet beds on his own grounds as a hobby. Among them is a flower clock which tells time with a face composed of foliage plants of the Victorian era: *santolina* (lavender cotton), *alternanthera,* and *iresine*. Mr. Sproul obtained the clockworks from an old sign and housed them underground in a metal box. *Photo by Hampfler Photo Studio*

North Carolina. The Palace, built in 1767–1770 as the Colonial capitol for Royal Governor William Tryon, and later used as the first state capitol of North Carolina, was destroyed by fire in 1798. Restoration was accomplished over a period of seven years (1952–1959) by the Tryon Palace Commission, supplemented with gifts and bequests of the late Mrs. James Edwin Latham. The great house with its gardens now stands as a replica of a great era.

With no records of previous gardens at Tryon Palace available, the commission constructed and planted gardens that were typical of those designed for English estates in the period from 1760 to 1770. Working from source material of that period, they faithfully reconstructed gardens designed as their English counterparts were, not for the public eye, but strictly for the enjoyment of the privileged few who could afford to maintain such estates; hence, they were called "privy" gardens.

Gardens of this period reflected a sophisticated, highly formalized return to nature. Straight entrance drives and garden paths were combined with gentle reverse curves, influenced by William Hogarth's "line of beauty." Wilderness areas flanking wide-open stretches of lawn were fashionable. The surprise elements of hidden circles, walks, and antique ornaments were also employed.

As productive space was limited in eighteenth century England, fruit trees were often espaliered and grown on garden walls. Flowers, vegetables, and herbs were intermingled in kitchen gardens.

The use of pleached allées, which provided long vistas, knots, and parterres combining color, texture, and pattern, the interspacing of flowers and greenery, the patterns of brick and stone walks and walls were all-important landscape elements in British gardens of this period and are utilized at Tryon Palace.

Fences of wrought iron and wood and colonnades, as well as outbuildings such as dovecotes, gazebos, and necessaries were employed for their ornamental as well as functional value. Statuary, urns, benches, sundials, wells, fountains, birdbaths, and fonts were among the many decorative devices that added materially to the air of formality and splendor these estates displayed.

During the late eighteenth century and extending well into the nineteenth century, many sea captains of New England coastal towns earned their livelihood transporting cargo to and from the "farthest points of the Rich East" and Europe as well. They built great houses which they furnished elegantly, and developed extensive gardens and grounds which contained many unusual ornaments. In some instances, the carved wooden figureheads from their ships eventually found a place in the garden.

Since the more elaborate properties were laid out in a grand manner, sculpture, made of sandstone or lead, which these seafaring men had seen in the great gardens of England, France, Italy, and Holland, inspired them to enjoy similar features in their own gardens. Wood was plentiful in America and ship carvers were numerous, with the result that many excellent figures were made. In 1793, John and Simeon Skillin, ranking wood-carvers of Boston at the time, produced a series of figures in wood for the garden and teahouse of Elias Hasket Derby in South Danvers. The standing figures measuring four and a half to five feet in height were executed with great skill and painted. They consisted of a shepherdess, a "Figure of Plenty," a gardener, and a "Hermit for a Garden." The shepherdess and the gardener surmounted the gables of the teahouse, flanked by a pair of handsome urns, while the "Figure of Plenty" had its place on a pedestal before the house. Samuel McIntire, Salem's noted architect and wood-carver, had designed and built the teahouse.

A climbing rose trained on a spindle fence serves as traditional decoration in many a dooryard along the eastern seaboard. *Photo by George Taloumis*

In the spirit of the Romantic movement in literature and the arts then current in England, the "Hermit" had a hermitage covered with bark which was especially built for him on a wooded part of the grounds. Eliza Southgate who visited the farm in 1802 described him "as a venerable old man seated in the center with a prayer book in one hand while the other supported his cheek, and rested on an old table." This amusing bit of whimsy, remote indeed from the traditional features of late eighteenth century New England estates, harked back to the then popular trend in England where grottoes, ruins, caves, temples, and similar unrelated follies were popular.

Perhaps the most fabulous collection of carved wooden figures ever assembled in America was that of "Lord" Timothy Dexter, a most eccentric character who lived on High Street in Newburyport, Massachusetts. In the early 1800s, he engaged Joseph Wilson, a local wood-carver, to make nearly forty images which were displayed across the front of his house and throughout his grounds on wooden pedestals, some of them fifteen feet high. A freestanding colonnade before the entrance was surmounted with figures, including one of Dexter himself, who claimed that he was "the first in the East, the first in the West and the greatest philosopher in the known world." The sculpture, much of it life-size, executed with notable skill in the tradition of ship figureheads, then in great demand, was gaudily painted and included such figures as Washington, Adams, Jefferson, Lord Nelson, William Pitt, Napoleon, as well as openmouthed lions, Adam and Eve in the garden, a lamb, a dog, a horse, a unicorn, and others. The curious came from miles around to see the marvelous display even though many of the lookers considered it sheer folly at best. Only a fragment of one piece is known to have survived.

Among the garden novelties of the period were the Chinese ceramic fishbowls, round or broadly oval, brought from Canton which were put out to catch rainwater or provide a place for goldfish. Some were made of stoneware, others of porcelain. At a later date, they were filled with soil and used as great flowerpots. Porcelain garden seats, or barrels (as they were sometimes called), were placed on porches or in the summerhouse. A pair flanked the entrance to the summerhouse of a Chestnut Street garden in Salem, Massachusetts, for many years. Great white clamshells from Sumatra, measuring two feet or more in length, could be found among the shrubs.

Ornate trellises inspired by the gardens of France and England supported roses, grapes, and other vines. Chinese Chippendale fences were the choice for enclosing some of the front yards. More ostentatious were the tastefully designed gates, gateposts, and fence posts surmounted with large urn-shaped finials which made the spindle fences true architectural gems, rich in detail. These handsome fences bounded the land on the town streets that enclosed the dooryard gardens and made the approaches to the square wooden houses charming and inviting.

When iron came into popular use for fences early in the nineteenth century, the designs and the construction bespoke the importance of building for permanence. Wrought iron featuring delicate scrollwork was utilized to make fences and gates of uncommon beauty. As the vogue for iron fences grew, more elaborate designs in the florid Victorian style were made possible with molds. Fancy cast-iron fences and equally elegant garden furniture were produced in quantity, not a little of which found its place in cemeteries. Granite and brownstone curbings were installed to support the fences. This was an era of solid construction.

Walks of brick, rotten rock, peastone, and tanbark make the sojourn into the box-bordered gardens pleasant and comfortable, for even then ladies wore thin-soled shoes. Usually, walks were edged with brick with trim borders of boxwood but if the owner was partial to Holland Gin, the round, brown, glazed jugs were upturned to make a border for a garden walk. One New England garden boasted walks bordered with nearly a thousand of these "gin-bottle" tiles.

Arbors, pergolas, summerhouses, and gazebos built of wood and trimly painted were often used either as terminal features at the end of a path or along the walk so that one might enjoy a glimpse of the garden in comfort on a hot day. (Suntan was not fashionable in those days.) There were toolsheds, barns, "necessaries" with paneled doors and bull's-eye glass in the windows, occasionally a countinghouse, and great hogsheads to catch rainwater. A weather vane was perched on the carriage-house cupola and most gardens had old sundials. A carved wooden eagle in gold leaf looked out to sea from the roof of Captain Nichols's carriage house in Salem. In an era when change came slowly, many of these gardens were maintained intact or nearly so for several generations. Even when paths and flower beds reverted to weeds and untamed growth, there remained enough in the way of original pattern and layout to suggest the former beauty and glory of many of these old gardens.

A ship's bell set on a sturdy cedar post in a Nahant garden now serves to call children and guests to meals. It has been used as a focal point in a naturalistic planting close to the water's edge where it is frequently hit by salt spray. *Photos by George Taloumis*

On a terrace overlooking the ocean in a small Maine town a sea nymph, in the form of a stern-board carving, looks out to sea. Although old carvings of this type are hard to come by, skilled craftsmen are making faithful and sometimes fanciful reproductions to meet the demand for Americana.

The seventeenth century garden adjoining the House of the Seven Gables, Salem, Massachusetts, built in 1668, is enclosed by a picket fence on the harbor side. A sundial is one of the few ornaments.

The old pump in the garden at Wheatland, Lancaster, Pennsylvania, home of James Buchanan, dates back to the early nineteenth century. *Photo by George Taloumis*

Patterned or knot gardens, remnants of an era when formalized design was popular, sustain interest at all seasons because of their evergreen outlines. Dwarf boxwood, teucrium, and lavender cotton were frequently used to create a desired pattern, many of which were derived from embroidery. This garden filled with hyacinths is bordered with dwarf hardy candytuft (*Iberis sempervirens*) Little Gem. The central pool is surrounded by walks of white crushed stone. *Photo by Paul E. Genereux*

The patterned or knot garden at the Jacob Wendell House, Portsmouth, New Hampshire, is a modest expression of a style that has enjoyed periodic revivals since the seventeenth century when it was fashionable in England. *Photo by Douglas Armsden*

An early nineteenth century summerhouse in the Safford House garden at the Essex Institute, Salem, Massachusetts. Sometimes these structures were placed halfway along a garden walk so that one might pass through, but more often they served as garden retreats. *Photo by S. T. Cahill*

During the latter part of the eighteenth century the vogue for ornamental fences was as solid as tradition in New England. Even garden paths were framed with well-proportioned wooden arches supported by square posts, which were ornamented with moldings. *Photo by Paul E. Genereux*

George Washington set this handsome brass sundial on a wooden pedestal in an oval grass plot in the center of the courtyard at Mount Vernon. It is surrounded by a railing of posts and chains similar to the originals described by Washington in his diary. *Photo by Marler—Mt. Vernon Ladies' Association*

Gardeners have a way of utilizing decorative objects of various kinds for garden ornament, but some attempts are less than successful. This cast-iron figure of Martha Washington was originally part of a "dumb and radiator and parlor stove" patented by Alonzo I. Blanchard of Albany, New York, in 1841. A companion figure portrayed George in a flowing toga. These hollow statues glowed when a fire was burned in a stove beneath them, providing a considerable amount of radiator heat. Few examples of this curious stove remain with the exception of those in private collections. A figure of George is displayed at Beauport in Gloucester, Martha stands in the garden of the Essex Institute at Salem, and both Martha and George may be seen in the Azalea Garden at Winterthur. *Photo by S. T. Cahill*

The dipping well in the kitchen garden at Mount Vernon and the French watering can are reminiscent of Old World gardens of the period. It was customary throughout Europe to expose water in great cisterns to the open air and sun, to soften it before it was used for plants. Washington's garden library was extensive and he practiced the art of growing fruits, flowers, and vegetables with great enthusiasm. Despite the fact that he was away from Mount Vernon for long periods of time, he wrote intimately to his gardener about the needs of his garden. *Photo, Mt. Vernon Ladies' Association*

The greenhouse, or orangerie, flanked by the servants' quarters, is situated on the north side of the flower garden at Mount Vernon. It is a faithful reconstruction of the original, built by Washington in 1785 and destroyed by fire in 1835. Eighteenth century greenhouses did not have glass roofs; this structure is built of brick with large windows to let in the southern sunlight. The box hedges in the foreground, planted in 1798, are the principal feature of the garden, creating a charming parterre. *Photo courtesy of Mt. Vernon Ladies' Association*

Highbush blueberry, Saint-John's-wort, junipers, sedum, and other plants, suited to seaside conditions, planted against a weathered redwood fence, make a setting for a carved wooden eagle perched on a weathered tree stump. A mulch of washed beach stones adds materially to the overall effect which is distinctive for its form, color, and texture. *Photo by George Taloumis*

The raised beds of the knot gardens at the House of the Seven Gables are held in place by wooden planks. *Photo by S. T. Cahill*

Since 1782, when it was adopted as our national emblem, the American eagle as a decorative motif has held precedence over all other designs. This example carved in wood in the nineteenth century is mounted above the entrance to an old carriage house. *Photo by Walton T. Crocker*

This handsome fence frames the dooryard of the Pierce-Nichols House, Salem, Massachusetts, which was built by Samuel McIntire in 1782 and is often described as the finest wooden structure of its period in New England. Old-time craftsmen used the term "spindle fences" to describe these sturdily made enclosures with their slender vertical spindles that pierce the broader horizontal rails (usually three) and are supported by stout square or boxed posts finished with moldings. The spacing of the rails and the spindles is prime proof of sound design as is the placement of the moldings on the posts. The urns which cap the post display richly carved festoons. The gate, with its graceful curve, believed to be a precise replica of the original, was restored nearly a half century ago. *Photos by Walton T. Crocker*

Long before it became the fashion to mount carved eagles over doors and on the sides of buildings, John Haley Bellamy (1836–1914) of Kittery Point, Maine, was turning out flocks of spread eagles and presenting them to his neighbors who promptly nailed them up on their houses and carriage sheds. These eagles were made of pine, painted white with touches of red and blue, and sometimes there were blue stars in the banners which they carried in their beaks or talons. Patriotic slogans were carved in the banners. Today the originals are sought at high prices but many excellent copies have been produced that are available at moderate cost. *Photo by Douglas Armsden*

A charming and original garden ornament is this antique Chinese tea-shop figure. Small metal figures such as these were used in front of tea shops in the mid-nineteenth century, and a few were still known to be in service before 1920 in parts of Brooklyn and Manhattan, New York. This gentleman, who stands approximately four feet tall, is depicted holding a fan in one hand and a lantern in the other. Attired in a richly detailed shirt that almost looks like real brocade, he probably once stood on a pedestal, as most tea figures did, with the name of the merchant whose wares he was advertising painted on the base. Sometimes he held a box of tea; occasionally a Chinese woman was depicted in a long gown. Besides being used as ornaments, these figures had other uses; one was adapted for use as a hitching post. *Photo by S. T. Cahill*

A cigar-store Indian, carved in the nineteenth century, stands in a natural setting on the grounds of the Elizabeth Perkins House, York, Maine. *Photo by Douglas Armsden*

The setting for this ancient figure of Venus with its paved forecourt is reminiscent of the manner in which classical sculpture was displayed in the open and along public ways in early Greek and Roman times. Both the ivy-covered brick column and the coppice growth featuring American dogwood in flower which form the background accentuate the atmosphere of the setting.

This piece of antique sculpture brought from Europe by the late Mrs. Francis B. Crowninshield is one of a number of rare garden ornaments that still repose in her garden at Eleutherean Mills, Montchanin, Delaware, now open to the public. *Photo by Gottlieb Hampfler*

2

SCULPTURE IN THE GARDEN

SCULPTURE has been described as an expression of the creative spirit of man. The use of statues in gardens may be considered the projection of the human personality into the realm of nature. In Greece, long before the Christian era, the sculptor's art was displayed in gardens and public ways, implying that a green background and open space were essential for an ideal setting. In the making of gardens, this practice has continued for several thousand years. In fact until the vogue for formal design was swept away a century or more ago, hardly a great garden was planned in the western world that did not have its share of sculpture. The human figure in its most ideal form was cut in stone or molded in lead and other metals. Some of the statues were life-size, others ranged from one-third to one-half normal height and, as terminal features for long vistas, impressive figures of heroic or colossal proportions were the vogue.

The rose, the acanthus, the grape, and other favorite flowers, leaves, and fruits noted for their distinctive form were either incised or molded on columns, panels, urns, seats, and other ornamental objects.

Even in the smallest garden, sculpture has a place. The right piece of the right size, suitably placed, is bound to lend interest. Human figures or those of animals used in a setting of foliage are ideal focal points where the eye may rest. The right size and shape, usually elevated on a pedestal, related to the scale of the planting and the entire setting, provide a humanized point of focus. The setting is equally important since the color, form, and texture of the background, thoughtfully chosen, enhance the overall effect. The choice of subjects is limited only by the imagination and the pocketbook of the owner. Classical subjects have been traditional favorites for centuries and are widely copied in several media. With the renewed interest in all the arts, many talented men and women have focused their attention on sculpture, and a fresh approach to the ancient art is unfolding.

Many pieces used today have an air of whimsy. Whatever the choice, the gardener needs to remember that sculpture, unlike a bench or a chair, a pot or an urn, has no functional use and is considered pure ornament. It needs to be so treated. Every era has had its "cutesy" figures either fantastic, grotesque, or purely eccentric in concept, or the so-called trick pieces that spouted water unexpectedly as one approached them.

Frequently, as in centuries past, pieces considered as works of art or those with exceptional appeal are copied in various media and, all too often, poor reproductions are made. Nothing can be more disappointing to the sensitive eye. On the other hand, a well-executed replica can bring great joy to the owner and beholder. Formerly, original sculpture was beyond the reach of the average gardener, but presently a surprising number of young sculptors are producing works of exceptional merit in both traditional and contemporary styles. These are often displayed at local art association exhibits and those sponsored by private galleries. As a result, it is often possible to obtain a truly noteworthy piece of original sculpture at modest cost.

Two antique Italian statues occupy prominent spots in the flower beds on the east side of Hawks Allée at Tryon Palace, North Carolina. They are among the five statues of Roman gods and goddesses, four of marble, one of terra-cotta, which came from the garden of the late Mrs. Louise du Pont Crowninshield in Delaware. *Photo by Herbert Rea. Courtesy, Tryon Palace Restoration*

Diminutive in scale, usually less than a foot tall, these pre-Columbian figures from Central America add an unusual note to a small garden or terrace, especially when placed on pedestals and set among groups of potted plants. *Photo, courtesy H. Kennard*

A youthful Diana, Goddess of the Wood, shown on a pedestal. *Photos by George Taloumis*

Pan playing on his pipes sits nestled among greenery at the edge of a terrace.

A Victorian white marble figure, draped in the classical tradition, makes a perfect focal point for a formal garden. Detail shown on page opposite. *Photo by Walton T. Crocker*

Classic figures cut in white marble, often life-size, were the vogue in the heyday of Victorian gardening. They were sometimes set in groves of trees or placed in gazebos. *Photo by Walton T. Crocker*

A figure of the Italian goddess Diana emerging from a simulated woodland serves as an effective focal point in a formal roof garden. The design of the wrought-iron bench in the foreground stems from the Italian Renaissance. Evergreen texture is supplied by the use of Japanese yew and English ivy which flourish in a high, raised planting area. A flowering crab apple breaks the sharpness of the corner. *Photo by George Taloumis*

Although this *Boy with a Dolphin* rests on a pedestal in a seaside garden, similar figures in stone, lead, or bronze are frequently used as focal points for fountains. *Photo by Stephen T. Cahill*

A charming statue of a merchild with a dolphin sits in the Langdon Memorial garden, Portsmouth, New Hampshire. *Photo by Douglas Armsden*

A majestic bronze statue, *Indian and Eagle,* by C. Paul Jennewein, stands in the Brookgreen Gardens, Murrells Inlet, South Carolina. Formerly the site of a rice plantation in the scenic Carolina Low Country, the estate was purchased in 1930 by Mr. and Mrs. Archer M. Huntington who restored and laid out the gardens as a museum and sanctuary for wildlife. Displayed throughout the grounds among magnificent live oaks and other native trees and plants is an outstanding collection, one of the largest in existence, of nineteenth and twentieth century American sculpture. It is considered a high honor among sculptors to have one's work exhibited there. Brookgreen Gardens serve as an inspiration for other gardeners, for the settings bring out the best in the sculptures while the latter enhance the area in which they are displayed. *Photo, courtesy Brookgreen Gardens*

A bronze fountain in a bog garden terminating a long vista. It features the god and goddess of love inspired by the Eros legend. Designed and executed by Anna Coleman Ladd. *Photo by S. T. Cahill*

A Merman

Figure of a Young Girl

Three bronze figures, life-size, designed and executed for the "Fountain of Life" by Anna Coleman Ladd (1878–1939), internationally known sculptor. They are now used as accents in a formal garden where the foliage textures of boxwood and Silver Mound artemisia complement the figures. *Photos by S. T. Cahill*

The Washerwoman, a bronze statue done in 1917 by Auguste Renoir, may be seen in the sculpture garden of the Museum of Modern Art in New York City. *Courtesy, The Museum of Modern Art, New York*

The Family Group, by Henry Moore, cast in bronze (1945–1949). *Courtesy, The Museum of Modern Art, New York*

Original sculptures, like this head of a woman cut in white marble in the early part of this century, are often discovered in unexpected places. The present owners found their treasure at an auction and placed it in a shady part of their garden against a rustic fence surrounded with vines and shrubs. It offers an element of surprise to the visitor who walks up the drive and turns to a side entrance. *Photo by Walton Crocker*

The rapture of a young child in an encounter with nature has been captured by Beverly Seamans in *Rain*. This bronze figure mounted on marble is twenty inches tall.

The Garden Sculpture of Beverly Seamans

WHEN a sculptor is also an active dirt gardener and the children she portrays play in her garden, the end result is often one of intimate vitality. Beverly Seamans of Marblehead chose to model her children and those of her friends in a series of characteristic poses that are so charmingly natural that it would seem that she had breathed life into her bronzes. All her children have busy hands. Her garden has evolved as a series of little vistas around a great ledge where wild flowers, ferns, and ground covers flourish, providing an ideal natural setting. When the children were small, she gardened with one eye on her trowel and whatever she was planting, while, with the other, she followed the youngsters as they romped over the rocks. Her memory became her camera. She knows the wonder and the joy of childhood. Her sculpture tells!

A young mermaid, modeled by Beverly Seamans, sits at the edge of a pool listening for the *Sound of the Sea*. The eighteen-inch figure of bronze on marble is piped for a fountain. *Photos by S. T. Cahill*

Waiting hopefully for a nibble, the young *Fisherman* by Beverly Seamans, done in bronze, mounted on travertine marble, sits at the edge of a pool against a background of pine. *Photo by S. T. Cahill*

Emerging from a wooded setting of ferns and evergreens is *Girl with Cat.* A bronze mounted on marble, this statue by Beverly Seamans stands eighteen inches high.

Peter gazes with rapt attention at a fish clutched in his hand. Beverly Seamans' eighteen-inch figure of bronze mounted on marble is piped for a fountain. *Photos by S. T. Cahill*

Clutching a fistful of sand, *Beach Baby* sits in rapt attention among the ferns. Piped for a fountain, the thirteen-inch bronze statue is the work of Beverly Seamans. *Photo by S. T. Cahill*

Jennie embodies the concentration and determination of a young child taking her first steps. She was done in bronze on marble by Beverly Seamans. *Photo by S. T. Cahill*

Saint Fiacre in action, a terra-cotta figure modeled by Lee Burnham.

A replica of the patron of gardeners, designed as a wall plaque. The original, in the Cloisters Collection in the Metropolitan Museum of New York, was made of alabaster in England in the fifteenth century. *Photo by P. Genereux*

SAINT FIACRE,
THE GARDENERS' PATRON

THE foremost patron of gardeners is a little-known Irish saint named Fiacre. In recent years his image has been used as a garden ornament, particularly in herb gardens. He lived in the seventh century and roamed from his native Ireland to preach to the heathen Gauls near Meaux, about twelve miles from Paris. With the approval of the local bishop, Faro, he chose a spot in the midst of a great forest and lived there as an anchorite. He cleared a spot in the wilderness and planted a garden of fruits, flowers, and vegetables.

This holy hermit, noted for his hospitality, his charity, and his urbanity, became widely known for his sanctity. Soon nobles, pilgrims, and serfs came to visit him seeking cures, comfort, and guidance. Thus his time was divided between contemplation and prayer, the care of his garden, and acts of charity.

For generations, gardeners in France observed the feast day of their patron saint on August 30 by attending services and decorating chapels dedicated to Saint Fiacre with an abundance of flowers. His memory is also preserved in parts of Scotland because of a tradition which formerly prevailed that Fiacre was a Scot by birth.

Saint Fiacre is also the patron of the Paris cabdrivers who adopted him because, in the seventeenth century, they transported hundreds of travelers to his chapel in coaches—hence the name *fiacre* for a cab in France.

Based on studies of drawings found in illuminated manuscripts and various statues of Fiacre made over a period of several centuries, Lee Burnham modeled her own concept of the gardeners' patron in terra-cotta. *Photo by W. T. Crocker*

Comparatively small in scale, this contemporary statue of Saint Francis of Assisi, patron of all nature, seems to belong in this summer garden. Depicted as a modest man who renounced his worldly goods to live a life of poverty and worship, Saint Francis was joined by his disciples to form the order of the Brothers Minor. His teachings are still carried on today by the Franciscan order. Universally known and loved, this saint is seen giving his blessing to all the birds and beasts of the world; hence he is an appropriate symbol for a garden, and his image is used in gardens in many parts of the world. *Photo by George Taloumis*

A tiny Mexican version of Saint Francis of Assisi, whose teaching had a great influence on the culture of that country, stands, in an attitude of prayer, over a fluted lead basin surrounded by myrtle and Christmas ferns. An espaliered flowering dogwood makes tracery against the wall. *Photo by George Taloumis*

Pan has been portrayed both as a mythological figure, part man and part goat, and as the incarnation of a youth in real life. Philip S. Sears has chosen the latter treatment in his bronze sculpture of Pan, the Greek god of the forests. *Photo by S. T. Cahill*

A shady nook in a suburban garden, where old yews spread their branches and ground cover makes a green carpet, suggested the setting for *Young Saint Francis* by Anne Jaggard Kopper. This noted sculptress who specialized in depicting moods and facial expressions of children often used her own children and grandchildren as models. Her work in lead and stone includes studies of children frolicking and in repose, as well as studies of animals and birds. *Photo by Donald Robinson*

AMORINI

AMORINI, putti, and merchildren were favorite subjects with Italian and French sculptors, especially in the seventeenth and eighteenth centuries when the use of garden statuary was in high fashion. Amorini may be described as chubby small children or cupids, usually nude, and often modeled with wings suggesting their origin from mythology. Putti is another Italian term for small boys or lads, portrayed nude or in swaddling bands, which were widely used in various art forms dating back to the fifteenth century. Merchildren are similar to both groups and usually associated with dolphins, nymphs, and the like. Bernard Berenson, the noted collector of Italian art, once wrote that Correggio had a passion for expressing a feeling of joy by painting putti at every opportunity.

Both amorini and putti are used to describe figures of curlyheaded children seen commonly in a variety of poses, mostly in action, often in playful mood, sometimes alone or in groups or with animals. Groups of four holding the symbols of the four seasons are fairly common and are reproduced frequently from molds in limestone, lead, and simulated stone.

The Four Seasons

Spring is usually portrayed as a little girl holding a garland or a basket of blossoms or sometimes a bird; while Summer is represented with a nude boy clasping a sheaf of wheat. Harvest fruits, especially grapes, the attributes of Autumn, are held by a curlyheaded boy, depicting the Autumn season, and Winter is represented by a nude little girl with a hood over her head and shoulders. Occasionally the figures are seated but for the most part they are posed in a standing position. As with most figures, pedestals are desirable for displaying them. *Photos by PIC*

41

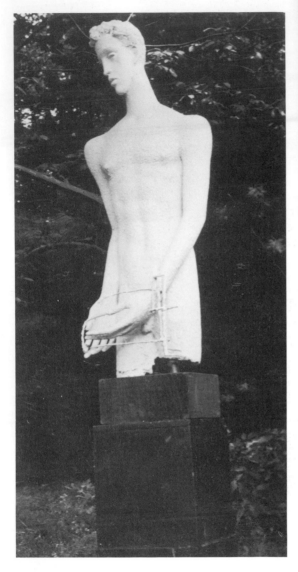

Entitled *The Unfinished Symphony*, this bust of Madame Serge Koussevitsky was carved in Tennessee marble by Peter P. Abate. Highly personalized sculpture is worthy of special attention when choosing a setting. *Courtesy, Pine Manor Junior College*

A feeling of love and tenderness pervades *The Pearl*, sculpted of Carrara marble by Peter P. Abate in 1953. This figure was executed by the artist while he was in Italy on a Prix de Rome. He climbed to the mountain quarry in the little town of Carrara in Tuscany and personally selected a block of marble from which he cut this sculpture. *The Pearl* was selected by the Metropolitan Museum of Art for exhibition. It measures thirty-six inches by thirty-one inches. *Photo by S. T. Cahill*

A direct plaster model of *Youth and His Dreams* by Peter P. Abate is a touching portrayal of a young man. Designed for bronze or white resin with welded bronze, it measures fifty three inches by fifteen inches and stands on a wooden base. The tranquil mood of this piece is reinforced by a wooded setting. *Photos by S. T. Cahill*

The Flower is rendered in steel, wood, and plaster on a heroic scale. Standing ten feet tall, this striking piece by Peter P. Abate is set at the edge of a grove of trees at the entrance to his driveway. Designed to be cast in bronze or white resin eventually, it is an eloquent floating figure, symbolic of the bilateral growth and development of a woman and a flower. Her gown is perforated to allow play of light and shadow. *Photo by S. T. Cahill*

A pair of bronze *Sea Gulls,* forty-four inches high, modeled by Beverly Seamans, seems so lifelike one almost expects to hear their cry. They are shown in a natural setting which serves to intensify their effect. *Photo by S. T. Cahill*

Peacocks cut in stone, molded in lead or iron, or modeled in pottery or stoneware are mute reminders of an earlier day when many a country garden along the Eastern seaboard and some town residences as well sported a muster of peacocks as highly ordered ornament. In *Old-time Gardens,* Alice Morse Earle described this exotic bird of handsome plumage as "a fitting tenant of old formal gardens" whose "panoply of iridescence and color makes many a gay flower bed pale." Native to India and Malay, the peacock was brought to America by way of England in the late eighteenth century. Yet, these vain creatures have their drawbacks; one is their habit of screeching loudly at the approach of dusk; another is their tendency as winter approaches to roost far from home in some high tree, usually inaccessible. Left alone in severe cold, they soon die. Thus, rescuing peacocks has never been considered great sport by those sent to retrieve them. A bird made of stone or metal eliminates all domestic problems.

Proudly mounted atop a brick gatepost is a carved English Bath-stone chanticleer. Each day he greets the dawn in the courtyard at the rear of the west wing of Tryon Palace. *Photo by Herbert Rea. Courtesy, Tryon Palace Restoration*

46

A piece cut from an old telephone pole resulted in this sturdy owl. A revival of interest in wood carving has produced many creditable examples which made suitable garden ornaments.

No source, however humble, should be overlooked by the collector. This intriguing cast-iron bird was discovered by his present owner in a flea market. Now he perches proudly on a garden fence.

Gift shops are a good source for garden ornaments. This copy of a very old Chinese duck reproduced in metal was found in a Cape Cod shop. *Photos by S. T. Cahill*

Eagles in flight, carved in wood which was gilded or painted, have been perching on the ridges of roofs and atop flagpoles for nearly two hundred years. This crisply carved specimen is within easy eye range so that it can be admired at close quarters. The skill required in carving a full-bodied, life-sized eagle signifies master craftsmanship.

A proud peacock is gallantly perched at a gateway to greet visitors. *Photos by Douglas Armsden*

Contemporary wrought-iron sculpture made in Spain is being used more widely in American gardens. The simplicity of form of many of these pieces transcends any definite style of design. They suggest a feeling for folk art with a modern flair. This bird is ideally scaled for use as a dramatic focal point. *Photo by S. T. Cahill*

A pair of roosters carved in wood, designed for use as gatepost finials or wall ornaments. For centuries, the rooster has been a favorite subject for weather vanes, and for roof and wall ornaments. *Photo by Ronald Rolo*

Sculptured squirrels guard the gateway to a garden. Small in scale, the pair complements the simple design of the low picket fence and gate. *Photo by George Taloumis*

Springtime lambs, made of bronze mounted on rough granite by Beverly Seamans, cavort in her garden. *Photos by S. T. Cahill*

The *Tortoise and Hare* nestled in a patch of bearberry eye each other warily. These figures, only five and six and one half inches high, were done in bronze on marble by Beverly Seamans.

Bayberry, beach grass, and rugosa roses with a clump of yucca for accent provide the most natural of settings for this approximately life-size slat goose decoy. Made of long, thin strips of wood, this type of open construction allowed the wind to blow through without upsetting the bird. These great decoys were so cumbersome that they were often left out-of-doors all year. In her book, *The Art of the Decoy,* Adele Earnest tells that Joseph Whiting Lincoln of Accord, Massachusetts, made many of these huge decoys, and he also carved heads for his neighbors. "Jo preferred to call them 'barrel geese' and found them most effective when used in conjunction with live decoys. In his day, 'honkers' were still legal." Slat geese have been used in New England since the early part of the nineteenth century. *Photo by George Taloumis*

Good sculpture, like good furniture, needs to be placed where it can be best enjoyed. A pair of whippets cast in bronze flank the entrance to a brick garden house. Belgian block and cut stone were used in paving. A large tree-form hibiscus flourishes in a "Caisson de Versailles" or copper-lined plant box, balanced by a weeping retinospora, far left. *Photo by Ronald Rolo*

A perennial favorite of children of all ages, *Peter Rabbit* by Beverly Seamans sits perched on a rock hoping that Farmer McGregor will not catch up with him. Peter stands twelve inches high and is made of bronze.

Every gardener worth his salt will declare that the only kind of rabbit to allow loose in a garden is one made of stone, cement, metal, wood, or pottery. This is Lucifer, once a pet of the noted sculptor Joseph Boulton, who modeled him. He is made of cast stone and stands twenty-seven inches high on a base twelve inches wide. A planting of dusty miller complements the setting. *Photo by Ronald Rolo*

Honey Bear, as endearing as his name, is made of bronze. Fourteen inches high, he was created by Beverly Seamans. *Photos by S. T. Cahill*

A fat, friendly frog made of molded concrete squats in a garden. *Photo by George Taloumis*

A baby bear in cast stone sits near a clump of prickly-spined yucca. Here is an ideal feature for a play area or a child's garden. It stands twenty-two inches high and is usually anchored in a concrete base. *Photo by Ronald Rolo*

This polished iron figure of a unicorn was originally painted black and used with a similar figure of a lion as part of the royal insignia of the British Crown. In bygone days these symbols were mounted above the entrances to English post offices. Now this one decorates the wall of a stone garden house. *Photo by S. T. Cahill*

Animal sculpture has a special place in gardens where there is ample space for a setting and suitable planting. The cast-bronze deer shown here in a natural landscape featuring a ground cover of bearberry and cotoneaster in the foreground and a background of evergreens and ornamented trees conveys the feeling of belonging to the site. *Photo by Ronald Rolo*

A pudgy cement hippopotamus serves as a step at the end of a garden path, suggesting that garden sculpture can be both useful and ornamental. *Photo by George Taloumis*

When a garden reflects the interests of its owner and he marks it with his own individuality, the results can be unforgettable. Robert A. Edwards designed an outdoor theatre in an open woodland at Paradise, Beverly, Massachusetts. He chose as a focal point a white marble bust of Euripedes, the noted Greek tragedian, and in front of it he placed a Corinthian capital made of limestone. The bust is a nineteenth century copy of one in the British Museum and the capital is an artifact brought from Rome more than fifty years ago. The trimly sheared hemlock hedges and the natural canopy formed by the dogwood, together with native ferns and wild flowers, complete the setting.

(Above) Detail of the limestone capital.
(Right) Detail of bust of Euripides. *Photos by S. T. Cahill*

A wellhead or well curb was a feature of every well-planned European garden in bygone days. This unique example is adapted from an ancient Corinthian limestone capital with a wrought-iron frame attached. Red cedars make the setting for it. The area at the base, originally paved in beach stones, has been somewhat overrun with lilies of the valley which form a green carpet in this shady retreat. *Photos by S. T. Cahill*

A Carrara marble baptismal font from an ancient Italian church, resplendent in its sculptured detail featuring an elongated oval basin. It is now used as a birdbath in a country garden.

A bas-relief panel in plaster adorns a brick wall in a city garden. *Photo by George Taloumis*

WROUGHT-IRON FENCE ON BRICK WALL

CHERUB WITH BASKET AGAINST AN AZALEA PLANTING

EAGLE

WROUGHT-IRON GARDEN BENCH

CHINESE PORCELAIN GARDEN
SEAT

TERRA-COTTA WALL PLAQUE

MOLDED IRON UNICORN

CAST-IRON FIGURE OF MARTHA WASHINGTON

LEAD FIGURE OF PAN

BRICK WALL IN A CITY GARDEN, POTTED PLANTS, AND A CERAMIC WALL PLAQUE

GRAVEL WALK

A tall carved antique font of pink marble (probably a baptismal font from an old cathedral) is the focal point of the east side of the Kellenberger Garden at Tryon Palace. It is surrounded by four rectangular beds filled with seasonal bloom, each containing a box tree and bordered by germander. In the background is a high wall of handsome brick covered with ivy. *Photo by Herbert Rea. Courtesy, Tryon Palace Restoration*

Much of the charm of garden ornament rests in the manner in which it is related to its setting. A weathered cement pedestal softened with woodbine supports a neatly sculptured Italian flower basket of limestone, aged by weather. Occasional pruning keeps the woodbine from concealing the object of interest. *Photo by Ronald Rolo*

In the Old World, pairs of fruit baskets, made of cast stone, or cut from limestone, were used frequently as finials on posts to define an entrance, on the tops of walls, or where a change of level occurred. The walk is of cut granite laid in sand.

An antique stone urn resting on a pedestal enhances the beauty of the grounds at Tryon Palace, New Bern, North Carolina. The estate was modeled after English prototypes of the mid-eighteenth century. *Photo by Herbert Rea. Tryon Palace Restoration*

The pineapple has fascinated gardeners since Columbus discovered it on the island of Guadeloupe during his second voyage in 1493. It was apparently brought to the West Indies by the Indians since it is a native of South America. It is a symbol of hospitality. This handsome sculptured specimen sits atop the post of a stone wall in a country garden. *Photo by George Taloumis*

Representing the *Repercussion* of dynamic movement in space, this contemporary sculpture by Peter P. Abate measures twenty-seven inches by twenty-nine inches and is made of welded steel with natural rust patina. Set on a wooden base, the figure is suitable for a garden or fountain and would make a stunning focal point in the center of a pool.

Reaching upward toward the sun, *Primavera,* made of steel and wood, is patinaed in developing spring colors to express budding growth. This striking piece of contemporary sculpture, ten feet tall, is by Peter P. Abate. *Photos by S. T. Cahill*

Carved from an old, hand-hewn oak log, this sculpture of *Mankind,* created by Peter P. Abate in 1947, is suspended on an iron base affixed on a swivel to turn with the wind and chained with iron to represent man as the chained victim of his environment since the beginning of time. The seventy-one-inch carving is shown against a forest setting, reinforcing its ruggedness and timeless quality. *Photo by S. T. Cahill*

A man-made mushroom fashioned from a section of railroad tie and the end of a New England granite boulder has been used as a finial on a stone wall. Inspiration for this unique garden ornament was gleaned from extensive study of Oriental garden art.

"Even a stone has a personality."
Photo by S. T. Cahill

Man in the Open Air, an early twentieth century bronze by Elie Nadelman, a gift to the Museum of Modern Art, New York City, by William S. Paley. *Courtesy, Museum of Modern Art, New York*

Sunlight and shadow highlight a wrought-iron gate flanked by two neatly cut stone posts. This country garden, reminiscent of the Old World, has mellowed with the years under the watchful eye of a truly great gardener. *Photo by George Taloumis*

3

FENCES AND GATES

Not only do "good fences make good neighbors," as Robert Frost reminds us, but they complete the setting of a house and its garden. Fences have been part and parcel of town and village living since the days of the early settlers, when sheep and cows had to be kept from eating up the herbs and the flowers that grew in their dooryard gardens. What became essential by way of necessity opened the way for an aesthetic touch. The fence soon related to the house as a frame to a picture. When a fence suggests the feeling of belonging to the house that it surrounds, as an old Cape Codder once remarked, "it's fittin' to be settin' there."

Fences serve to mark boundaries, to give privacy, to screen unsightly areas, or to divide the various units of a property. Yet, this need for utility need not exclude an eye for pleasing design and appropriateness. The fence is an extension of the architecture of the house, and its design as well as the material of which it is made should reflect the same feeling. Since people like to look through fences, or over them, or to catch a glimpse through the gate of what lies beyond, fences need to be friendly. While solid barriers are sometimes needed, the spaced-picket or spaced-board fence that allows for sunlight and air circulation is preferable, especially when there is a garden within. Planning, designing, and building the right fence for your property is worth the time and expense involved. Cost is a prime factor since most fences must be custom made even though, in some instances, standard parts are readily obtainable.

When wood is used, details to be considered include the kind of wood best suited, adequate foundations for the posts, weatherproofing, color (paint or stain), and the amount and cost of maintenance required. To reflect good craftsmanship, construction needs to be sturdy to withstand weather and to be trim in appearance as well. Since moisture is the prime enemy of wood, preservatives and paint or stain are usually essential. These are best applied before the fence is assembled to assure the longest possible life-span. Skilled craftsmen are aware of these factors and the property owner needs to realize their impact. The selection of the right kind of wood cannot be overemphasized. The more durable kinds like redwood, cypress, red and white cedar, black locust, and others are more costly than pine, hemlock, spruce, and fir. Often wood from the latter group is used where it will not come in contact with the ground.

63

Both fence and gate are in the Chinese Chippendale manner, often referred to as Chinese lattice, which was fashionable in eighteenth century England. At the time, lattice effects were also a part of furniture design and the motif was repeated in garden seats and benches as well as fences. The trend spread to America, where garden fences made even a century later had these same patterns. Examples are to be found in Colonial Williamsburg, in New England seaport towns, in California gardens, and sometimes where eighteenth century houses are reproduced. *Photo by George Taloumis*

The kitchen garden at Mount Vernon, faithfully reconstructed from the gardening books used by George Washington, has many interesting ornamental features typical of eighteenth century English prototypes. To the left is a handsome picket fence with posts capped by delicate finials, a noteworthy architectural feature that linked the gatehouse with the enclosed garden. The octagonal gatehouse, which serves as a "necessary," flanks one side of a sturdy wooden gate. A spacious brick walk and a solidly built wall are other interesting features, both useful and ornamental. *Photo courtesy of Mt. Vernon Ladies' Association*

Sturdy construction assures permanence. Cut granite set in cement makes a solid wall to support an equally well built picket fence with square posts, allowing for filtered sunlight and good air circulation. Beyond the fence in the dooryard is a trimly designed wellhead which harmonizes with the architecture of the house. Sound design of a functional structure provides a handsome ornament. *Photo by Douglas Armsden*

Privacy as well as a setting for the garden is the result with a brick wall, heightened and lightened in its effect by the use of latticework. Even the boxed posts that link the lattice panels suggest an effect of permanence. *Photos by George Taloumis*

A terraced effect on two levels focuses attention on the use of metal for garden ornaments. The wrought-iron railing above the granite wall is securely anchored with gracefully curved brackets protruding like gargoyles in silhouette. Cast-iron chairs are arranged for comfort near the French doors. On the lower level, the wall serves as an appropriate background for a small fountain that spills water from a satyr mask into an eighteenth century lead cistern—a type commonly used in Old World gardens to catch rainwater. Weather has given the molded decoration a rich patina. A pair of unusual lead wall containers filled with geraniums flank the cistern, together with two richly textured mounds of plantain lily. Pots of geraniums and ivy add color to the setting, complete with a brick-paved foreground.

In West Coast gardens where redwood is used extensively, fences are often designed in an imaginative way. This example described as a translucent screen combines redwood with variegated stained glass. *Photo by Harlow. Courtesy of California Redwood Association*

An English hurdle fence of sturdy design separates a meadow from a lawn area. A paperbark maple with its orange exfoliating bark lends a note of interest. *Photos by George Taloumis*

A balustrade from an elaborate nineteenth century house, rescued from a wrecking company, lends a decorative effect to a city garden.

A redwood fence becomes an effective and decorative screen by spacing the uprights with one-inch blocks of varying widths. The play of light and shadow adds to its eye appeal. Robert W. Stevens, designer. *Photo, California Redwood Association*

Decorative panels of contrasting color relieve the monotony of a solid redwood fence. John Staley, landscape architect. *Photo by Dennis Galloway. Courtesy of California Redwood Association*

Wrought-iron grillwork topping a low stone wall provides an openwork screen to enclose a terrace. Several panels of scrollwork were incorporated in the enclosure which ties a low-slung house and terrace into a gently rolling landscape that rises sharply in the rear of the property. The result is a delightful outdoor room. *Photo by Donald Robinson*

A contemporary fence made of redwood lattice backed with translucent plastic, designed by Robert Cornwall, provides an unusual and decorative screen. Filtered light that penetrates through the plastic is not only an aid to the shrubs and ground cover but adds to their eye appeal. Podocarpus makes an effective accent against the fence of this West Coast garden. In colder areas, columnar yews allowed to grow loosely would create a similar effect. *Photo by Morley Baer. Courtesy of California Redwood Association*

Sapling fences with their reddish brown bark are especially desirable when naturalistic effects are sought. While they make ideal windbreaks, the spaces between the saplings allow for air circulation in a garden. *Photo by George Taloumis*

Post and rail fences are usually of rough wood construction but this fence has granite posts and mahogany rails which have weathered to silvery gray. Designed by Planning & Research Associates Inc. *Photos by George Taloumis*

The open-board fence in various designs makes an attractive boundary marker, especially suited to suburban and country areas.

The lush bloom of azaleas makes a foamy background for the scrollwork of wrought iron. A capped brick wall supports the fence. *Photo by Walton T. Crocker*

The use of round-topped pickets of graduated height and square, urn-capped posts give this high wooden fence a crisp finished appearance in a small city garden where privacy and air circulation are needed. *Photo by S. T. Cahill*

The bark of several oriental pines offers more than the ordinary eye appeal at all seasons of the year, but from frosttime to early spring it attracts particular attention. This group of Japanese red pines in Ritsurin Park, Takamatsu, protected by an intriguing bamboo fence, brings into sharp focus the beauty of tree bark. *Photo by George Taloumis*

When a fence is built of top-grade materials and carefully painted by master craftsmen, it becomes a fitting frame for the house and grounds. This spindle fence based on a nineteenth century prototype is distinctive for its simplicity and detail. The trim caps on the posts, the graceful curves that flank them and the raised, fluted panels are architectural refinements seldom seen in present-day designs. *Photos by Walton T. Crocker*

Interesting patterns are produced by the bold shadows cast on basket-weave fencing. This type of enclosure ensures privacy while admitting sunlight and allowing air circulation. The step effect created by placing the sections on an inclining slope add interest to this property. *Courtesy, Walpole Woodworkers, Inc.*

Beyond this white painted fence with its fancy pickets and its arched gate lies a view of the Atlantic Ocean. *Photo by George Taloumis*

The subtropical lushness of growth, in itself a study in textures, is accentuated to a high degree by a gate of simple design, a sturdy dry wall, and substantial paving. *Photo by George Taloumis*

This Chinese garden gate flanked by two native red cedars, has been an intimate part of a charming naturalistic New England garden for nearly half a century. It is one of those unusual bits of Oriental garden art that seems to belong where it has been placed. Even bereft of its carving, its general design and structure may well serve as inspiration for a present-day gate maker. Nearby is a pool where lotus thrives, blooms, and sets seed each year. A large part of the charm of many old gardens rests in discovering them. *Photos by George Taloumis*

One of the most widely photographed gates in all New England is that of the Wedding Cake House in Kennebunkport, Maine. When this two-story brick house was transformed with Gothic ginger-bread practically every known device of the scroll-saw era was employed in the most fanciful way. The gate alone contains enough design elements to make several of distinct style. The spindle fence was a favorite with skilled carpenters in New England in the nineteenth century. *Photo by Douglas Armsden*

This well-proportioned low gate with its pleasing curve and its unusual bell seems to say "Welcome." Trimly turned urns cap the posts, and the simple picket fence complements the house it surrounds.

Tall, stately, painted wooden posts and a pair of peacocks made of cast stone frame a noble elm standing against a background of blue water in a Maine garden. *Photo by Douglas Armsden*

Reminiscent of Spanish wrought-iron craftsmanship, the scrollwork pattern of this tastefully proportioned, painted wooden gate bespeaks more than ordinary skill. *Photo by George Taloumis*

A decorative wrought-iron gate and high brick wall, topped with ornamental urns of classical design, are typical of those found on large estates built in eighteenth century England. The entrance to the formal gardens at the Governor's Palace in Williamsburg, Virginia, shown here, and that of the gardens at Tryon, New Bern, North Carolina, are prime examples of artistry. *Courtesy, Colonial Williamsburg*

The owner of this house need not worry about dogs digging up his garden. A weighted ball and chain automatically ensures that the gate will close. Each post and spindle of this wooden fence at Colonial Williamsburg ends in a small carved finial. Fencing was first required in Williamsburg by an ordinance of 1704. Present-day crews are kept busy maintaining more than seven miles of fencing. *Courtesy, Colonial Williamsburg*

4

THE PERGOLA

THE pergola had its origin in Italy and has been used extensively in Spanish gardens for centuries. In more recent times, it has become a pleasant feature of many English and American gardens. Essentially the pergola functioned to form a shaded passageway from one building to another or as a connecting link between features in a garden. To support the growth of woody vines, it needs to be of sturdy construction with posts or columns made of wood, stone, or brick. The beams extending across the top are either finished or left rustic. Sometimes strapping or trelliswork is used along the sides to encourage vine growth upward.

Numerous variations are found today, including some with built-in seats. Sometimes finials are used for ornament over the ends. The most appealing pergolas are those tastefully planted with roses and clematis so trained and thinned as to let light filter through to encourage the growth of lilies and other plants within the framework.

Wisteria, which is used commonly on pergolas, is a vigorous twining vine producing an abundance of heavy growth. It needs frequent pruning not only to keep it within bounds, but also to prevent it from overpowering and weakening the structure.

Paths under these structures need paving with stone or brick or the textured effect of fine gravel (peastone). To belong to its setting, a pergola needs to fit its location and be so designed that it is high enough and wide enough for the traffic expected.

A graceful pleached allée in the Tryon Palace gardens provides shade as well as a long sweeping vista to the Trent River. Yaupon, a native Southern holly, is trained over a lofty arch, and among the plants lining the marl walk are ferns, periwinkles, ivy, hosta, ajuga, and iris. A stone bench and an antique urn, mounted on a sandstone pedestal, provide a focal point beyond. *Photo by Herbert Rea*

The twining treelike growth of an old wisteria trained over an extensive arbor spanning a zigzag stone bridge lends a feeling of age and maturity to the setting. Constant pruning of suckers and top growth helps to accentuate the woody character of this handsome ornamental vine. Sturdy but simple construction is another example of Japanese know-how in building an arbor. *Photo by George Taloumis*

A view of the Potomac River is seen through the north colonnade at Mount Vernon. The colonnade was a prime feature of Old World formal gardens in the sixteenth and seventeenth centuries. More solid in construction than a pergola, with its molded columns and railings and arches topped with keystones, it is related architecturally to the main house, providing a covered walkway that leads to the outbuildings. Coral honeysuckle vines soften the wall above the arches and add a colorful touch through the summer months. *Courtesy, Mt. Vernon Ladies' Association*

Hanging pots filled with ivy geraniums provide color in a California garden and decoration for a contemporary pergola that has many of the features of the lathhouse. *Photo by George Taloumis*

This unusual arbor in the Thomas Bailey Aldrich garden in Portsmouth, New Hampshire, is attached to the house and joined to a fence at the left. It serves not only as a framework for climbing plants but also as an extension of the fence, forming an architectural and ornamental enclosure for the garden. The gracefully curved arches and decorative urns contrast pleasingly with the simple clapboarded exterior of the house. The louvred lower portion of the arbor allows for air circulation, yet maintains privacy and screens a side entrance to the house. *Photo by Douglas Armsden*

A pleached allée of hornbeam in the garden of the Governor's Palace at Williamsburg, Virginia, photographed in early spring before the new foliage unfolded. Shaded walks, a feature of eighteenth century gardens in Europe and the British Isles, are seldom seen today. From late autumn until early spring, the framework and twig growth show to advantage. *Photo by George Taloumis*

The pleached allée of hornbeam in full leaf at the Palace Gardens, Williamsburg, Virginia. *Courtesy, Colonial Williamsburg*

Turf steps are seldom seen in present-day gardens because of the maintenance required. These at the Moffat-Ladd House, Portsmouth, New Hampshire, were built more than a hundred years ago. The vine-covered arbor with its pleasing curved lines makes an ideal site from which to view the flower garden below. *Photo by Douglas Armsden*

A cascade of color provided by laburnum (golden chain tree) and lavender wisteria covers the top of an arbor in the First Church garden in Salem, Massachusetts. A modified version of the arbor in the Ropes Mansion Garden, this structure provides cover for a garden seat. Derived from the old English word "herbere," meaning a place to grow herbs, the arbor later evolved into a form of summerhouse. *Photo by Elizabeth Freeman*

A fascinating study in perspective is provided as one looks down a long vista upon entering this arbor in the garden of the Governor John Langdon Memorial (1784), in Portsmouth, New Hampshire. Of simple wood construction, the framework acts as a support for climbing roses. The shadows cast by the framework and foliage heighten its dramatic effect and when the roses are in bloom, the interplay of light, shadow, and color makes this structure an outstanding garden ornament. *Photo by Douglas Armsden*

A sturdy yet gracefully designed wooden arbor based on an early nineteenth century model, capped with an urn finial, supports a wisteria and serves as the entrance to the garden of the Ropes Mansion in Salem, Massachusetts. *Photo by Walton T. Crocker*

Interesting shadow patterns are cast by the slats of a long redwood shelter designed by Robert Jones. The posts also serve as a trellis for roses and other climbing plants. *Photo by George Lyons. Courtesy, California Redwood Association*

Slatted pergola construction for the roof of a small paved porch serves as an ideal support for a large-flowering clematis which seems to belong here. *Photo by George Taloumis*

5

THE GAZEBO

In the sixteenth century when the great gardens of the Old World were enclosed by walls to keep out intruders and wild animals, it was customary to build a sturdy enclosed structure in one or more corners of the wall, complete with roof and walls with openings on all sides so that the women and children might gaze upon the wilder landscape. This was the beginning of the gazebo. Later, structures erected in strategic parts of the garden were built where the family might go to read, rest, practice on the violin, visit, or contemplate. These buildings afforded privacy, protection from the weather, and a change from the rustle and bustle of the house. Gradually, gazebos became simpler in construction with solid or open roofs and windowed or open sidewalls. Shrubs and small trees were sometimes planted around them and vines were allowed to cover them with tracery. Or, they stood in some strategic part of the garden, at the end of a path, or partway along it where the family might tarry. Summerhouses and garden houses were other names attached to these structures which might be square, round, octagonal, hexagonal, or some variation of these forms. When viewed from a distance, they lent an architectural feeling to the setting and helped to set the scale for the plantings near them.

This gazebo, originally the cupola of a mansion, now sits nestled among the trees at the edge of a garden. *Photos by George Taloumis*

Of simple and sturdy design, a country summerhouse provides a cool place to rest one's weary feet while viewing the garden in the foreground.

A screened gazebo of colonial design, surmounted by an eagle, stands in the garden of the Pickering House in Salem, Massachusetts. *Photo by Elizabeth Freeman*

A gazebo of eighteenth century designs provides a pleasant spot to tarry while enjoying the Benjamin Waller garden. *Photo by Thomas L. Williams. Courtesy, Colonial Williamsburg*

Small wooden summerhouses with latticework screening and built-in benches may be seen in old New England gardens. *Photo by George Taloumis. Courtesy, Essex Institute*

A poolside redwood shelter resembles a pagoda in form. Its continuous bench provides a shady spot when one wishes to escape the heat of the sun. *Courtesy, California Redwood Association*

A tiny octagonal gazebo is nestled against a brick wall in the west corner of the garden at Mount Vernon. Like the Mansion and its other outbuildings, this structure is built of beveled wooden siding, finished with sand on white paint to imitate stone. Perched on the red-shingled roof is a finial like those seen on fences and gateposts elsewhere on the grounds. Originally, this building served as a schoolhouse; presumably the students were better able to concentrate on their lessons when removed from the hustle and bustle of the main house. *Courtesy, Mt. Vernon Ladies' Association*

A redwood garden shelter designed by Robert Tetlow offers privacy as well as protection in case of rain. *Photo by Phil Palmer. Courtesy, California Redwood Association*

An eighteenth century garden restored by the Pennsylvania Horticultural Society at its headquarters near Independence Square, Philadelphia, features a summerhouse with arbor attached. The use of latticework in a Chinese pattern suggests the influence of chinoiserie so prevalent at the time. Trimly edged beds and walks covered with washed gravel define the pattern of the garden. *Pennsylvania Horticultural Society*

A contemporary redwood A-frame shelter designed by Armand Ramirez serves as the focal point of a garden and also offers protection from sun and wind. *Courtesy, California Redwood Association*

Nestled behind a high brick wall in the Stanley House garden at Tryon Palace is a gazebo, providing shade and privacy on a warm summer afternoon. The formal arrangement of the brick wall, fountain, and shrubbery contrasts with the natural growth of trees beyond the wall. *Photo by Herbert Rea. Courtesy, Tryon Palace Restoration*

GARDEN ARCH OF WOOD (NINETEENTH CENTURY TYPE), WALK OF PEASTONE (WASHED GRAVEL), AND FLOWER BEDS EDGED WITH BRICK

MARBLE FIGURE OF CHILD WITH BIRD USED AS A TERMINAL FEATURE

SIMULATED STONE RABBIT

VICTORIAN CAT IN SIMULATED STONE

SAINT FIACRE, PATRON OF GARDENERS

CARVED PINE MASK

CHINESE STONEWARE PEDESTAL

BRONZE URN

PORCELAIN JARDINIERE

CHINESE PORCELAIN GARDEN SEAT

PANSIES IN A TERRA-COTTA STRAWBERRY JAR

NINETEENTH CENTURY SUMMERHOUSE

RED AND WHITE FUCHSIA IN A TERRA-ROSA POT

A simple A-frame shelter of redwood with a canvas awning provides the perfect spot for children to play or rest on a hot summer day. *Photos by Ken Molino. Courtesy, California Redwood Association*

A California redwood gazebo of contemporary design is an inviting spot in which to read or converse.

A small orange tree in a seventeenth-century, Dutch, two-handled flowerpot, probably a foot in diameter. This type of container was popular for nearly two hundred years in European gardens. Pots of this type were made of terra-cotta and sometimes given a glazed finish. A patterned garden enclosed by a lattice fence completes the painting *Spring,* one of four of *The Seasons* by David Teniers the Younger.

6

POTS, WINDOW BOXES, AND OTHER CONTAINERS

OF all the ornaments commonly used in gardens, the flowerpot holds first place, since practically all cultivated plants are grown in pots in one stage of development or another. A flowerpot is a portable garden, allowing for handsome effects according to size. Until a few decades ago, pots, tubs, and window boxes were the three common kinds of containers used in gardens. But as hobbyists with plants expanded their interests, necessity, the mother of invention, marshaled the use of every conceivable kind of object that would hold earth. Plants had been grown in tin cans since they were first made. Now there is no limit to what may be used. Coal hods, washboilers, discarded automobile tires, old iron and soapstone sinks, wheelbarrows, washtubs, iron cooking pots, sleighs, and other outmoded or discarded articles have found a new use. A lady at a Maine summer resort assembled a sizable group of old-fashioned bathtubs and filled them with flowering plants. Even the lowly chamber pot has been put to similar use. For the most part, these containers offer little in the way of aesthetic appeal and belong in the same class with the cheap sculptured ornaments which the British call garden monstrosities and monsters.

Clay pots, plain or decorated in line or in sculptured form, have notable eye appeal. The shape of the typical tapered flowerpot undoubtedly had its origin in the Bronze Age burial urn as did the bucket, the dye pot, and other useful household utensils. For centuries, clay has been an easy-to-use and common material for pots. Queen Hatshepsut had her favorite plants in pots in her garden along the Nile nearly fifteen hundred years before the Christian era.

Indoors or out, wherever it rests, a pot of flowers serves as one of nature's most pleasant ornaments. Most gardeners would say that a pot is not an ornament; rather it is a necessity for all who enjoy growing things. A pot may become an ornament when it is designed with a large lip, ridged lines, sculptured encrustations such as masks, garlands, handles, and the like. More than a thousand years ago, Chinese potters decorated their wares with colored glazes and naturalistic designs, featuring flowers, birds, and animals. In the Renaissance gardens throughout Europe, pots were often made with a pair of handles and modeled to suggest the form of classical urns. The craftsman's skill was ever present in certain handmade touches, variations, and irregularities which suggest that many of them were thrown on a potter's wheel rather than molded. Notions of the sizes and shapes are best derived from a study of prints of the period. The passion for growing tender exotics including oranges, lemons, pineapples, and other tropical plants led to the extensive use of tubs, boxes, and pots measuring two feet in diameter or more. Often, the tubs and large rectangular boxes were made with an eye to paneling, moldings, decorative knobs, and footings. Even the plainest of containers had a decorative aspect by reason of its graceful tapering or its clean lines.

Ceramic bowl-shaped containers, similar to this example in simulated stone, were widely used in China more than a thousand years ago. Generous size and pleasing shape allow for the use of large masses of a favorite ornamental plant as with the pansies shown in this photograph. Cobb Blake who crafted it calls this container a pansy pot. It measures twenty-four inches across with a depth of six inches and is modeled so that the subtle scalloped variations in the roundness of its form have a ceramic refinement. Soft green coloring and a sand-textured surface add to its eye appeal. *Photo by George Taloumis*

Plant containers used on walls may be of unglazed terra-cotta, metal, glazed pottery, or plastic. Because most of them are comparatively small, they are seldom satisfactory unless watered frequently. Semicircular plastic containers, approximately nine inches long, available in white, green, and several mottled effects, retain moisture satisfactorily for two to three days in partial shade. They are inexpensive and easy to handle. The container shown here is filled with semperflorens begonias which bloom constantly. *Photo by Walton T. Crocker*

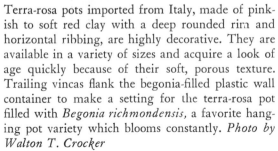

Terra-rosa pots imported from Italy, made of pinkish to soft red clay with a deep rounded rim and horizontal ribbing, are highly decorative. They are available in a variety of sizes and acquire a look of age quickly because of their soft, porous texture. Trailing vincas flank the begonia-filled plastic wall container to make a setting for the terra-rosa pot filled with *Begonia richmondensis,* a favorite hanging pot variety which blooms constantly. *Photo by Walton T. Crocker*

Brick paving and an ivy-covered brick wall make an attractive setting for a pot of flourishing geraniums resting on a well-weathered pedestal. *Photo by George Taloumis*

Magnificent ornamental urns, used in pairs, richly decorated with amorini, acanthus leaves, and egg and dart molding, flank the garden path at the Governor's Palace at Williamsburg, Virginia. The love of formal classical order in the mid-eighteenth century is reflected not only in the design of the building, but in the landscape planting as well, which features an abundance of clipped evergreens. *Photo, courtesy Colonial Williamsburg*

Narrow, light green foliage typical of many of the species of bamboo makes a pleasing contrast with the dark green of English ivy clinging to the wall. *Photo by Ronald Rolo*

94

A pair of metal planters, painted black, designed like epergnes, filled with runnerless strawberries to suggest tiered topiary, flank this entrance. Sculptured stone figures used as finials lend additional height. A well-balanced effect results from a pair of white iron benches, and two groups of potted pink geraniums provide abundant color. Paving stones set in sod make an inviting approach walk. The runnerless strawberry, variety Baron Solemacher, which blooms continuously through the summer months, is noted for its small clusters of colorful red fruits. Another feature of this plant is its fine-toothed foliage which retains a fresh appearance throughout the growing season. *Photos by George Taloumis*

The entrance to a handkerchief-size city garden is made inviting with a collection of "cottage-garden" potted plants to provide color and interest in a surprisingly small area where every square foot counts. The plants include fuchsia, lobelia, browallia, and geraniums as well as terra-cotta pans filled with sempervivums. The tall pot holds Swedish myrtle.

A small palm (thrinax) in an ornamental clay pot casts a shadow that emphasizes the beauty of both.

The color of the sand-textured, paved surface is repeated in the stoneware container which is filled with fragrant-leaved lemon verbena. This old-time tender shrub has been cultivated in herb gardens for centuries. Here is a notable example of a handsome green ornament flourishing in a well-chosen container that fits the site and softens the corner of the garden house. The play of light and shadow provides dramatic emphasis.

Podocarpus, a tender, long-needled, evergreen tree, related to the yew and native to Japan, is prized for its somewhat irregular and picturesque manner of growth. An ideal pot plant, its popularity is on the rise for indoor decoration because of its shade tolerance and easy culture. The container, of Oriental design, as well as the setting, harmonizes nicely.

A roof garden enclosed by a brick wall superimposed with a rustic fence makes a pleasant setting for herbs, rhubarb, and espaliered fruit trees grown in containers. *Photo by Paul E. Genereux*

An inexpensive molded cement pot measuring fourteen inches in diameter by seven inches high, filled with fingerbowl geraniums.

A bowl-shaped container of contemporary design filled with bougainvillea happily situated on the stone wall of a Hawaiian garden. Frangipani and a palm provide the background. Although bougainvillea is a rampant tropical vine, noted for its rapid and vigorous growth, it can be controlled for container use. *Photo by George Taloumis*

A summer plant room in a city garden made by using one unit of a two-car garage. Concrete building blocks provide support for slabs of marble used for shelving, with shelf brackets used above. Two-by-fours attached to the upper timbers and a sheet of plastic form the background. An ideal arrangement for summering tender houseplants and for propagating, this improvised plant room also serves as an appropriate background for an extensive pot garden. *Photo by Walton T. Crocker*

A tree geranium in a wooden tub and a wrought-iron garden chair decorate an entrance. *Photo by George Taloumis*

The rough-textured, simulated stone container in soft green, filled with geraniums and surrounded by pots of English ivy, provides an ideal setting for a portable garden on the brick ramp of a garage not used in summer. *Photo by George Taloumis*

Pansies in a glazed, clay-colored strawberry jar, approximately eighteen inches tall, make a striking terrace ornament for full sun or light shade. By turning the container every three or four days, feeding at two-week intervals, watering as needed, and removing dead flowers promptly (to prevent seed formation), this container provided continuous color and pleasure for its owners for ten weeks beginning in early spring. *Photo by Walton T. Crocker*

Plants and the containers that hold them become colorful ornaments on several levels in a city garden. The large molded container of rough-textured, soft green, simulated stone holds a gardenia. Standard clay pots were used for the hibiscus. A metal container on the gate is filled with German ivy. The second-story, removable, wooden window box, tastefully designed and bracketed to fit the site, is filled with pink geraniums and browallia. Copper lining was provided for the window box.

Light and shadow as well as sun and shade are factors to conjure with in city gardens. The brick pattern has not been lost with painting and the black wrought-iron balcony with its scroll design provides a lacy effect against the whiteness. Potted geraniums flourish in the brightest light, with a tree fuchsia, a yew, and a wisteria for the shady area. *Photos by George Taloumis*

A pair of iron urns painted white highlight a seaside garden where white picket fences and a white arbor are used to frame the flower beds and lawn. The box-bordered brick path and the great circular millstone softened with thyme are other decorative features. *Photos by George Taloumis*

Collections of plants like this one featuring cacti and succulents with a few foliage plants for variety have strong eye appeal when skillfully arranged to accentuate form, texture, and color. The metal table and weathered rustic fence help to create a restful overall effect on this sunny terrace.

A hanging basket suspended from an iron bracket filled with variegated flowering maple relieves the monotony of a high stockade fence, making it a more pleasing frame for a city garden. *Photo by George Taloumis*

THE POTTER'S ART

Gardens make ideal galleries for the potter's art, providing space and light as well as a background of grass, walks, and foliage where form, detail, and sculptured effects show to best advantage. Visitors to the Old World seldom fail to be impressed with the great gardens of France, Italy, Spain, the Netherlands, and Great Britain, where urns, vases, oil jars, and pots of every size and description are a major part of the ornament. An extensive array of traditional forms has been perpetuated, beginning with the Minoan amphora, from Knossus at Crete, a two-handled pottery vessel used to hold wine, oil, and other liquids, fashioned from clay more than twenty-five hundred years before the Christian era. The roots of the cult of the beautiful are so deeply imbedded in the human spirit that craftsmen at periodic intervals in human history have been inspired to re-create these classic shapes. As with costumes, modifications in shape and detail make it possible to fix dates. Thus, the garden ornaments we enjoy today are linked with a way of life, with houses and with gardens, that have long since passed into oblivion.

At the turn of this century, Eric Soderholtz, a Swedish immigrant, sailed to the Mediterranean islands from Boston to take photographs of architecture and gardens. There, he became fascinated by the pottery objects he saw. Upon his return to America he built a summer cottage at West Gouldsboro, Maine, a small town near Bar Harbor. For nearly forty years, using forms made with the aid of photographs, sketches, and notes, he produced an amazing collection of garden ornaments using cement, sand, and other materials to create the classic shapes resembling the texture of stone which he had seen in the Old World. His talent was soon discovered and the demand for his craftsmanship was great, not only to supply ornaments for the great gardens at Bar Harbor and Newport but elsewhere along the eastern seaboard and across the country. One commission for ornaments, shipped by schooner from Bar Harbor, weighed fifty-two tons. Architectural societies honored him and the Chicago Art Institute gave him an award for his urns in 1913. In recent years, his work has been revived by Cobb Blake at Camden, Maine, who has mastered the techniques of Eric Soderholtz. The wavy lines, the subtle curves, the delicate details of decoration, the texture all reveal the marks of masterful craftsmanship. Some have an earthy look, while others suggest the polish of Renaissance art. Comparisons made with early Chinese ceramics show a notable Oriental influence in the design of some of the containers. The containers shown on these pages, for the most part, were photographed more than half a century ago, without plants, to show the beauty of form. *Photos, courtesy of Duane Doolittle and Cobb Blake.*

This tapered bowl requires a pedestal or plate beneath it to accentuate the beauty of its form. Possibilities for placement include its use as a central feature or focal point where several walks or paths meet so that it may be viewed in the round, or against a background of evergreen foliage.

Large pail-shaped pots originally made to hold orange trees are ideal for standard fuchsias, hibiscus, large foliage plants, and various kinds of trees and shrubs. Used singly, in pairs, or in groups they add dimension to a large terrace or patio.

Italian in design with a pleasingly rounded rim, this tailored pot with its clean-cut lines requires a much taller and more impressive mass of foliage than it holds.

The shape, decoration, finish and attached stand suggest one of several traditional designs used for ceramic fishbowls in China. By selecting the right plant or group of plants for this simulated stone pot, its intrinsic beauty can be enhanced greatly.

Urns, singly or in pairs, lend an air of elegance to a garden. Although linked usually with great gardens, laid out with allées, parterres, sweeping lawns, and the like, an urn of the right size and shape, or a pair, can be thoughtfully placed even in a small garden to set the tone of the place. When cemeteries were modernized a decade or two ago, cast-iron urns were easy to come by for little money. Not so now, but excellent copies in iron, simulated stone, and other materials are available.

The irregularly formed rim and rough texture and finish of this vessel give it the effect of ancient pottery such as the Koreans made more than a thousand years ago. Plant containers of this sort with a primitive feeling are the result of skill* in the art of modeling a pot.

With or without planting this low bowl-shaped container of smooth-finished stone has distinct eye appeal. Given ample space so that the beauty of its form can be seen from a distance, it becomes an object of distinct decorative quality. *Photo, courtesy Duane Doolittle and Cobb Blake*

Garden designers in the eighteenth century turned to the ancients for their inspiration in selecting ornaments. The graceful forms of Greek and Roman oil jars, unearthed by archaeologists, were a prime source of decoration. Often these were placed either on the ground against a background of foliage or on low pedestals in a flower garden for accent. Size in relation to site is important to their effectiveness and placement. *Photo, courtesy Duane Doolittle and Cobb Blake*

Wherever used, the window box becomes a source of color in all seasons. Spring-flowering bulbs, forget-me-nots, and pansies provide early effects. Begonias followed by chrysanthemums serve for summer and autumn. Winter, the longest span of all, is brightened with bittersweet, bayberry, and greens. Moldings used on wooden boxes lend eye appeal and a finished effect as well as added strength to the construction. Custom-made boxes like this one are well worth the investment.

On a more modest scale, fragrant-leaved peppermint geraniums, heliotrope, and lantana do their bit to express the meaning of simplicity in ornament. *Photos by George Taloumis*

Strawberries thrive in the pot on the table, while trumpet lilies hold the center of attention. To the right, a terra-rosa pot of geraniums and a strawberry jar brimful of petunias give this bluestone terrace an appealing air. *Photo by George Taloumis*

A box of luxuriant foliage and flowers becomes a miniature garden bed to embellish the drawing room window of a Beacon Hill mansion. Plant materials for this partly shaded site include coleus, patient Lucy, and English ivy. *Photo by George Taloumis*

REDWOOD CONTAINERS

THE heartwood of redwood is used for making a wide variety of planter boxes. This material has proved to be a prime source of inspiration to architects and landscape architects, particularly on the West Coast where it is used extensively. In other sections of the country its use has widened considerably in the past decade. The natural preservatives in the redwood repel insect and fungi damage occasioned by constant watering. Kiln drying has produced a wood that endures extremes of temperature and moisture. Redwood is by no means inexpensive but it is worth what it costs. Since other woods stained to resemble it are commonly sold, the buyer should beware of substitutes. Various water repellants as well as light and heavy-bodied stains are used to retain its natural color or to change it. Left to weather naturally, redwood eventually becomes driftwood gray, a pleasant complement to evergreens and flowering plants.

Redwood lends itself to a variety of sizes and shapes so that containers can be built to fit the specific needs of deep-rooted trees and shrubs or groups of plants desired for a single container. Ready-made or custom-built dollies allow for easy movement of heavy containers, thus creating a portable garden. Provision for drainage by drilling holes or proper spacing of bottom boards is essential. All nails and metal attachments used must be corrosion resistant. The California Redwood Association recommends the use of stainless steel, aluminum alloy, or top-quality, hot-dipped galvanized nails and fasteners to avoid chemical reactions, resulting when metals come in contact with redwood extractives. Otherwise, black streaks appear on the wood. Also, it should be realized that the extractives will stain concrete patios and similar surfaces unless precautions are taken. The inside of the planter may be lined with polyethylene film, or the inner surface may be coated with a tar substance. Instead, a water repellant may be used on the inside surface, provided a two-week period is allowed before planting for the dissipation of toxic agents. To avoid stains, perhaps the easiest approach is to use a metal pan or tray under the container for the first two or three waterings.

Redwood tubs, planter boxes, and hanging baskets are produced in a variety of standard sizes, but these may not always fit specific locations. Custom-made containers can be designed to accentuate vertical or horizontal lines, or to place emphasis on an architectural detail or motif. Although ideally suited to contemporary architectural settings, redwood containers blend admirably with practically every kind of architecture, however traditional. In essence, many of the designs in use today had their origin in Oriental gardens a thousand years or more ago. Square containers were in use throughout Europe in the Renaissance. The point of specially designed containers is to build the right size and shape for the right place, fitting it to the right plant, tree, or shrub.

Photographs, courtesy California Redwood Association.

A redwood container supports a Russian olive on a New York City roof garden where it thrives in sun and wind. The silvery foliage softens the starkness of the walls and fence. *Photo by George Taloumis*

This bowllike planter, three feet square, allowing for a six-inch depth of soil, is well suited to various kinds of flowering plants, herbs, or a miniature garden of succulents. The redwood floor and railing of the sun deck, as well as the folding canvas-back chair, create a setting well suited to relaxation. Container designed by William Van Fleet. *Photo by Larry Coy*

A weathered redwood tub of standard design holds a camellia. The chopped bark mulch, reddish patio blocks (cement), and brick step are part of the picture. *Photo by George Taloumis*

The pebble-filled tray adds greatly to the architectural effect of this well-conceived planter which could accommodate a foliage mass of more generous proportions. Designed by Ted Osmundson.

Hexagonal containers had their origin in the Orient. The pebble-filled tray and the picturesque pine echo the same feeling. *Photos, courtesy California Redwood Association*

Repetition of forms is evident in the containers and the paving pattern. The upright habit of the big-scale shubs suggests columnar form desirable to lend height to the low-slung house. Even the row of shrubs under the windows serves effectively to point up the significance of the overall ornamental result. *Photo, California Redwood Association*

The old Chinese adage "a picture is worth ten thousand words" fits this photograph precisely. Empty or planted, these redwood containers fit the site. Charles W. Callister and Henry Herold, architects. *Photograph by Philip L. Molten*

TECHNIQUES FOR GROWING PLANTS IN CONTAINERS

ALTHOUGH this book is concerned primarily with the various kinds of garden ornaments, complements, and accessories and their uses in the garden, precluding how-to-do-it procedures relating to general garden practice, a brief description of the techniques of container gardening is included since containers are the most widely used of all garden ornaments.

A window box, a wooden tub, a large flowerpot, or some makeshift receptacle—even a painted tin can—often serves the novice who would have a garden despite the limitations of his surroundings. Even with a minimum of direct sunlight, window ledges, terraces, porches, balconies, or fire escapes can provide settings for a single plant, a collection, or a miniature garden. Once the requirements of adequate drainage and fertile soil are met, the novice selects plants according to their light requirements and his adventure begins. Some beginners, determined to start from "scratch," sow seeds or obtain cuttings which they root in water or a soil mixture. However, the majority, eager for immediate results, start with potted plants.

Choosing the Container. For easy maintenance and sturdy growth, containers must be large enough to hold a sufficient amount of soil so that the roots of the plants will not dry out quickly. Flowerpots or containers less than ten inches in diameter are usually not practical, although they can be used. The smaller the container, the more frequently it must be watered. Deep containers are preferable to shallow types. There are so many kinds of plant containers available in garden shops and nurseries that the choice is wide enough to meet the demands of the most discriminating gardener. Durability is a prime requisite. Any container chosen must be wide enough and heavy enough so that when filled with soil, it will not tip over in heavy wind. On the other hand, unless given a permanent place, the container should not be so large as to require more than one person to handle it. Sometimes, containers are made to order with wheels attached, or redwood platforms with attached wheels may be purchased for those that are to be moved occasionally.

To prolong their use, wooden containers need to be treated with a wood preservative inside and out before painting. Redwood containers last considerably longer if given treatment on both surfaces with a wood preservative. When the bottoms of wooden containers rot, after several years of use, they may be replaced with hardware wire and lined with black plastic paper.

New clay pots (both the common and the fancy French and Italian types) need to be thoroughly soaked before they are used so that the porous clay can absorb an ample supply of water. Otherwise, a dry clay pot absorbs water needed by plant roots from the soil.

Metal and wooden containers with painted surfaces need to be repainted every few years to preserve them and to enhance their appearance. For this reason, those made of redwood or cypress are often preferred since they take on a pleasing natural appearance as they weather.

Providing Drainage. Adequate drainage is as essential for success as is good soil. Whether made of wood or metal, a window box needs a three-quarter-inch hole in the bottom for each foot of length. Additional holes can be made by boring or punching. The same principle holds for tubs and other types of wooden planters. Clay pots and most types of ceramic, plastic, fiber-glass, and metal containers are designed with openings in the bottom or sides. To provide adequate drainage, cover each opening with a flat stone or a piece of broken pot, concave side down. Then add a one-inch layer of broken pots, small stones, or coarse gravel. To keep the soil from washing through, use a piece of burlap or a layer of sphagnum moss to cover the drainage holes. Containers without openings, especially those that are nonporous, demand special attention. Provide for twice as much drainage material (such as crocks and pebbles) as recommended for those with holes. Otherwise, during seasons of prolonged rain, the soil becomes waterlogged, and results may prove disappointing.

Preparing soil. Fertile soil with the capacity to hold moisture is a basic requirement for obtaining good results in any type of planter. Adequate organic matter is needed in the soil for moisture retention, since soil in containers dries out quickly when exposed to sun and wind. Plant food, absorbed by water in the soil and made available to plants through their roots, is not effective in dry soil. Prepared soil may be obtained from greenhouse or garden centers. Or, use the following formula:

> 2 parts garden loam
> 1 part (salt-free) builder's sand
> 1 part peat moss, leaf mold, or prepared humus.

To this mixture add 1 tablespoon of bone meal for each 10-inch potful or a 5-inch potful of bone meal for each bushel. Bone meal supplies phosphorus and potash which plants require and is made slowly available when added this way. Some gardeners use a complete fertilizer with low nitrogen content such as 5-10-10—or its equivalent.

Planting. Moist, workable soil is the ideal medium for planting. Fill the container with enough soil to allow space for the root ball of each plant. Then set the plant or plants in place, filling the space around them with prepared soil. Firm the soil around the plants with your hands, using a stick or trowel handle to eliminate air pockets. Then soak the container thoroughly to settle the entire soil mass and eliminate any remaining air pockets. Additional soil may be needed. The soil level in any container must be at least an inch to an inch and one half below the sides of the container to allow for adequate watering and mulching.

Feeding. Container-grown plants respond readily to feeding with a complete fertilizer. Apply it every two to three weeks, following the instructions on the container. Fertilizer may be scattered on the surface of the soil and watered in or mixed with water. Foliar feeding (feeding by spraying plant food on leaves) is also good practice, and many gardeners are dedicated to this method. Various kinds of liquid plant food are available, including such materials as fish oil emulsion. Watering after feeding is essential to make plant food available to the roots. Beware of fertilizer overdoses, which usually produce an overabundance of foliage at the expense of flowers.

Maintenance. Pinching plants to induce branching and removing dead flowers and yellowing or damaged foliage are the essentials of maintenance. Occasional pruning to improve appearance and staking tall plants are other points to remember. In essence, container gardening, unlike planting in beds and borders, is a showcase procedure. Unkempt plants are sad to behold and not worth having.

Watering. While overwatering is practically impossible in gardens, soil in containers may become saturated during heavy rains, hence, the need for adequate drainage. Waterlogged soil prevents the movement of air which is essential to healthy growth. When the condition persists for long periods, roots decay and plants die. During hot and windy weather, most containers may require daily watering. If small containers are used, both morning and evening soakings may be needed. A mulch of crushed stone, pebbles, or wood chips—at least an inch deep—is a practical way of conserving moisture. To soak adequately, a container that has drainage openings, enough water must be applied so that the excess drains away at the base. Containers without openings need to be watered more carefully. It is far better to have container-grown plants show signs of wilting than to water too frequently.

Window Boxes. For uncounted thousands of plant lovers who reside in cities, window box gardening is the only means of growing plants. During the spring they may be filled with spring flowering bulbs, pansies, forget-me-nots, primroses, and others. Through the summer and fall months, geraniums, petunias, coleus, patient Lucy, and a dozen other kinds of summer flowers are an unending source of pleasure. In late fall, chrysanthemums fill the bill, and during the winter cut greens and showy berries provide new variety.

Boxes vary in size according to the window, usually 2½ to 3½ feet long. Adequate depth and width are vital to good growth. A box at least eight inches deep and ten inches wide allows for enough soil and root space. An inch or two more in both dimensions is all to the good. Wooden boxes are preferred to metal because metal absorbs and holds heat during prolonged periods of hot weather. The soil, in turn, becomes warmer than is desirable for the plant roots. Materials used may be redwood, cypress, cedar, or white pine; boards at least one inch thick should be used. If the boxes are to be painted, both the inner and outer surfaces need treatment with a wood preservative. Even if a natural finish is desired, treating the wood is important. A window box filled with moist soil and plants is sufficiently heavy to warrant sturdy support in the way of brackets and bolts or lag screws.

Drainage, soil preparation, watering, feeding, and maintenance are the same as for other types of containers.

Mulching. To conserve moisture in containers, use mulches such as peastone, washed gravel of larger than peastone size, beach stones (washed thoroughly to remove salt), or chopped bark (available in varying sizes) to cover the soil surface of the container. To be effective any mulch used in containers needs to be at least one inch deep.

Present-day imports from Italy include reproductions of a wide array of garden ornaments. Among them are terra-cotta pots, plain and decorated, in a variety of sizes, which exemplify the principle that functional objects when thoughtfully designed are aesthetically pleasing. The restrained use of molded swags of flowers on this pail-shaped pot is accentuated by a molded ridged lip and raised bands of terra-cotta. *Photo by Ronald Rolo*

7

DOVECOTES AND BIRDBATHS

Dovecotes

THE pigeon house or columbarium was a favorite structure in the great gardens of England and other European countries in Tudor times. These buildings, according to the time in which they were built, were either square, round, or octagonal and made of wood, brick, or stone. A gabled or domed roof, topped with a cupola, together with various openings for the pigeons on the sides, made them decidedly picturesque. Miniature structures of similar form, placed on high walls or on sturdy posts, were commonplace in the more modest gardens in an era when pigeons supplied a convenient form of fresh meat during the winter months. Dovecotes in the Chinese manner, pagodalike houses, came into fashion in English gardens as a result of the writings of Sir William Chambers in the eighteenth century. Some of these aviaries—which were highly elaborate in design and exceedingly charming in their lush green settings—rated as prime curiosities. Today, dovecotes are by no means commonplace in gardens, but where they are used, they provide great delight for children and adults as well, especially when fine breeds of pigeons are kept.

A dovecote made of weathered wood supported on a column or sturdy pole and complete with a roof of thatch has been a favorite cottage garden ornament in Europe for centuries. Sometimes these structures are made entirely of wood and painted in a light color. Contemporary designs featuring a series of small boxlike houses attached on all four sides of a post are seen occasionally. *Photo by Ronald Rolo*

A martin house has tiny openings to discourage larger birds. Like the toolhouse beyond, it has a shingled roof. *Photo by George Taloumis*

A bird feeder is an addition to any garden and a must for all bird lovers. *Photo by McFarland*

Birdbaths

BIRDS have been synonymous with flowers since gardens were first planted, but the birdbath as a highly functional garden ornament is of comparatively recent origin. Providing fresh water in which birds may bathe brings its share of rewards. Birds not only devour many kinds of menacing insects, but they bring life, action, and color into the garden at all seasons of the year. To be sure, some kinds raid berry patches, grape arbors, and fruit trees, but on the whole their merits far outweigh their depredations.

Our forebears knew the value of birds in gardens. In the days when every garden worthy of the name had its fountain, pool, or some other water feature, there was no need for a special basin for the birds since there was water aplenty. In the wild, nature provided watering places for them—pools, streams, running brooks, waterfalls—as well as the natural basins in ledges and rocks formed in the glacial age.

As cities and towns grew and expanded, woodlands, meadows, and pastures disappeared and gardens became smaller and fewer in number. To lure birds, natural history societies, nature clubs, and the Audubon Society movement focused attention on providing places for them to nest and feed. Berry-bearing shrubs and trees were planted in gardens to provide them with food to encourage their presence. The vogue for birdhouses became popular and feeders of various types were designed. Similarly, the need for birdbaths in gardens became important.

Birdbaths made of lead or simulated stone, many of them tastefully designed, were conspicuous features of gardens designed at the beginning of the present century. Not all the birdbaths used in gardens today are as well designed as one would wish. Mass production has resulted in a sameness of form and finish that leaves much to be desired. Often the pedestals are clumsy and the basins are lacking in gracefulness of form. It takes more than casual shopping to find a well-designed birdbath these days. However, there is an ever-growing group of skilled craftsmen whose work is worth considering. Then, too, many firms who specialize in quality garden ornaments offer a variety of good designs. These are well worth the cost.

One of the early designs for a birdbath made of simulated stone, the leaflike shape shows to good advantage on its classic base. *Photo by Duane Doolittle and Cobb Blake*

A block of rough granite with a basin hollowed out makes a favorite bathing and drinking place for a flock of English fantail pigeons that roost and breed in the gabled end of a nearby garden house. *Photo by Ronald Rolo*

Looking like a giant mushroom, a birdbath cut of rough granite rests on a block of the same material. The encrusted lichens, the variegated pachysandra, and a good-sized holly tree complete the setting.

A stone basin in the Generiffe Gardens in Granada, Spain, inspired the designer of this birdbath which was made by Cobb Blake at the Ragged Sailor, Camden, Maine, and Tiburon, California. It is one of several garden ornaments in the author's garden. A cast-cement figure of spring, one of the "Four Seasons," set on a columnar pedestal, towers above the masses of speciosum lilies which bring abundant color to the azalea garden in high summer. *Photo by Photographic Illustrators Corporation*

A rock with a depression in its surface makes a perfect natural birdbath, especially when it is placed in a setting surrounded by ground covers and wild flowers. *Photos by Ronald Rolo*

High-flying city birds bathe in a basin supported by a cupid. Flanked by two small statues of fantail pigeons, the bath is surrounded by yews, chrysanthemums, geraniums, and English ivy.

A small sculptured scallop shell with a bird on its edge serves as a birdbath on a terrace planted with thyme. *Photos by George Taloumis*

A Sumatra clamshell, brought to New England in the early nineteenth century, surrounded by variegated English ivy, makes an unusual birthbath.

Flanked by tulips in the spring, a charming fountain (adapted to serve as a birdbath) typical of those used on eighteenth century English estates, stands in the center of the west side of the Kellenberger Garden at Tryon Palace. Water flows into the basin from a jet and spills into the pool below. Trellised vines soften the brick wall and building. Seasonal flowers provide color throughout the growing season. *Photos by Herbert Rea. Courtesy, Tryon Palace Restoration*

A dovecote and well on the grounds of Tryon Palace were two features found on mid-eighteenth century estates in England. Made of brick, as are the main buildings, the dovecote contains two life-like lead pigeons in its upper windows.

The well dates back to the founding of New Bern, North Carolina, in 1710, or perhaps earlier. It is referred to as "The Wishing Well" by schoolchildren who drop coins into it in hopes that their wishes will come true.

A wooden decoy, perched on the edge of a cut granite trough waits for his feathered friends to stop for a bath. *Photo by George Taloumis*

8

GARDEN FURNITURE

SINCE the art of garden making dates back to the early days of civilization, we shall never know who made the first collection of garden furniture. In 660 B.C. the Assyrian King Ashurbanipal was depicted reclining on a high chaise in the royal garden feasting with his queen who is seated on a chair. At a later date the Chinese developed a much more comfortable lounge chair for garden use. It was known popularly as the drunkard's chair since many of the mandarins used these chairs after imbibing too much wine. Ancient Persian and Greek prints show country houses and gardens featuring benches. Pliny the Younger, Roman author and orator, writing in A.D. 62 described a setting in his garden at Tusci as follows: "At the upper end is a semicircular bench of white marble, shaded with a vine which is trained upon four small pillars of Carystian marble." He goes on to say, "Fronting the bench stands a chamber of lustrous marble, whose doors project and open upon a lawn; from its upper and lower windows the eye ranges upward or downward over other spaces of verdure. In different quarters are disposed several marble seats, which serve as so many reliefs after one is wearied with walking." Archaeologists working at Pompeii excavated gardens indicating that they were designed for outdoor living and dining.

In medieval Europe garden parties were festive occasions. An early sixteenth century Brussels tapestry shows guests at a garden party playing cards and chess. Gardens were also a pleasant place to assemble for various games, music, dancing, bathing. Turf seats afforded a place to rest or a bench could be found in a nearby arbor. The marble table with its pedestal base was a permanent piece of furniture in many gardens. Paintings and woodcuts of the period show them either with the "apple of redemption" or the bread and wine symbolic of the Holy Eucharist.

During the Renaissance, balls, feasts, masquerades, and all sorts of frivolity took place in the great gardens of the Italian countryside. At the Villa of Castello, perhaps the most magnificent garden of its period, there was a great holm oak supporting a tree house reached by a winding staircase. Here one could see a marble table containing a marble vase "from which a little fountain of water spurted."

Among the garden antiques that remain are several types of metal garden seats and settees made in the late eighteenth century. Made of wrought iron, they are notably graceful in form and suggest a feeling of airy lightness and delicacy. Furthermore, they were designed with sitters in mind and when supplied with waterproof seat cushions are most comfortable for resting weary feet, far more so than the stiff-backed, short-seated forms produced in the Victorian era.

A number of Sheraton designs fit this description also. Rare among them is the iron tree bench, sometimes made in two parts to fit around a tree trunk. Cast-iron replicas, typically Victorian in design and often painted white, were much more common. These are reproduced by several manufacturers and are available at moderate cost. Metal furniture produced today varies in design and quality from cheap to first class. The surest way to find the kind that suits you best is to try the chair before you purchase it. Comfort is far more important than the eye appeal that some styles offer.

Holly hedges clipped to varying heights provide an effective setting for a Chinese Chippendale bench of eighteenth century design in the Palace Garden at Colonial Williamsburg. *Colonial Williamsburg*

This low redwood bench was designed to harmonize with the serenity of a Japanese garden by the sea. *Photos by George Taloumis*

An elegant, nineteenth century cast-iron bench of generous proportions is placed so one can enjoy the spring garden.

In the eighteenth century, garden furniture was designed with an eye to comfort as well as appearance. This bench of generous proportions in the Norton Cole Garden is flanked by a pair of boxwood bushes with a background of clipped evergreens. *Courtesy, Colonial Williamsburg*

Rough granite slabs are built into a slope to provide a naturalistic effect as well as a pleasant spot in which to pause in a rock garden.

A rustic wooden garden bench on wheels is flanked by pinxster bloom azaleas and tubs of geraniums. The bench design had its counterpart in English gardens of an earlier century.

The clean straight lines of the terrace and flower beds are reinforced by a concrete bench. *Photos by George Taloumis*

Strength and solidity are imparted by a contemporary garden bench. The strong horizontal lines of the bench contrast pleasingly with the planting of pachysandra, and the magnolia and the Boston ivy on the wall.

Sturdy wooden chairs fit the site and provide a pleasing contrast to stone used in their surroundings. A foundation planting of evergreen euonymus and petunias softens the effect of a hard wall surface. *Photos by George Taloumis*

A wrought-iron bench provides a pleasant place to tarry in a garden where ground covers, flowering shrubs, and evergreens are featured. *Photo, courtesy of John Burbidge*

Garden furniture today is available in a variety of sizes, shapes, and styles. Contemporary pieces, light-weight, carefree, and simple in appearance, can easily be arranged in groups and moved back and forth from terrace to lawn for parties, informal dining, or relaxing. *Photo, courtesy of Brown-Jordan Co.*

In a shady setting, one would be tempted to lounge on a graceful chaise of bronze-colored metal upholstered with vinyl. Lightweight pieces that are easy to move about are a must for a terrace or sun deck.
Photo, courtesy of Brown-Jordan Co.

Poolside furniture can be both weather resistant and attractive as evidenced by a grouping of tubular aluminum pieces upholstered in a diagonal pattern with vinyl strapping. A cleverly designed screen on a frame provides relief from the heat of the noonday sun. *Photos, courtesy of Brown-Jordan Co.*

Furniture that would be equally at home indoors or out is available in almost every style from the most casual to the most elegant. White cast-iron chairs, accented with gaily striped seats, and a white-framed glass-topped table add an air of formality to a brick terrace.

Wrought-iron furniture, designed in the French tradition with delicate tracery and a graceful silhouette as well as a floral pattern on the washable cushions, complements the use of potted and hanging plants. *Photo, courtesy of Meadowcraft*

Well-made aluminum garden furniture is maintenance free and easily portable. The classic good looks of a group of pieces make it a welcome addition to an outside terrace. *Photos, courtesy of Meadowcraft*

The graceful curves of a set of carefree, comfortable aluminum furniture contrast pleasingly with the vertical and horizontal lines of the brick wall in the background.

Comfortable, lightweight furniture, uncluttered in appearance, easy to maintain and to move is a "must" for a poolside terrace. An umbrella table provides shade for a poolside snack or chat on a warm day.

Sun worshippers and sometime loungers enjoy the simple styling and comfort of aluminum furniture upholstered with vinyl strapping on a poolside deck.

A rattan sedan chair with a foam rubber seat and a matching glass-topped table lend an Eastern touch to a patio. *Photo, Willow and Reed, Inc.*

Grassy and paved areas form an interesting pattern, their rectangular and square shapes echoed in the design of the contemporary wooden garden furniture. The bamboo effect in the framework of the lounge chairs complements the oriental planting in the background. A Japanese black pine adds contrasting texture. *Photos by George Taloumis*

Furniture that fits well into any setting, from the backyard terrace to the beach, is a boon to contemporary living. Originally designed for the tropics, a West Indies chair made of heavy duty aluminum tubing with a baked enamel finish and covered with vinyl lacing is durable as well as attractive. *Photo, courtesy of Tropitone*

Sturdy adjustable wooden lounge chairs, which are easily moved, covered with weatherproof cushions, provide comfort for sunbathing. A clipped willow oak and espaliered tupelo add an interesting background effect to the sod terrace studded with flagstone. The diamond-pattern trellis is yet another feature of this restful outdoor room.

A brick terrace of simple pattern lined with boxwood provides a setting for outdoor dining and is enhanced by a graceful wrought-iron table and chairs, embellished with scrollwork and fruit.

A tranquil spot for relaxation is found in a bluestone terrace screened by fence and foliage. The furniture is simple but sturdy in design, weatherproof, and comfortable as well as pleasing to the eye. *Photos by George Taloumis*

An aura of the Far East is imparted by a solid aluminum lounge chair with stylized bamboo treatment on the frame. Stout vinyl strapping, available in a variety of colors, makes this chair impervious to the elements. *Photo, courtesy of Scroll, Inc.*

A semicircular wooden bench and a small round table typical of garden furniture used in the 1920s and earlier, of sturdy construction, designed to fit into the corner of a garden. *Photo by McFarland*

Molded contour-form aluminum chairs in an informal conversational grouping add just the right touch to a terrace. *Photos by George Taloumis*

Beneath a great European beech, random-cut stone has been used to pave an outdoor room. Victorian cast-iron furniture, painted white, appropriate to the era in which the beech was planted, competes for attention with the sunlight which filters through the branches. *Photo by George Taloumis*

In this small garden walled and paved with old water-struck brick, the walls are softened with vines as well as hanging pots of trailing vinca and a ceramic wall plaque done in sculptured collage by John R. Burbidge. Sculptural collage involves the use of terra-cotta, glazed or natural, in the creation of plaques for decorative effects on walls, fences, garden structures, and for indoor use as well. A terra-rosa clay pot filled with *Begonia richmondensis* adds a note of pink which complements the old brick. *Photo by Walton R. Crocker*

9

GARDEN WALLS

In lieu of fences or hedges, walls have been used for centuries to enclose gardens. Stone, brick, and cement are the materials which have been in common use. The Chinese used ceramic tiles and elaborate coping to ornament their walls. Panels of openwork tiles, often of contrasting color, were devised with intricate patterns. Some were placed low enough in a wall to afford a look-see into the garden. Walls afforded protection and privacy as well as a background for what grew within. Brick walls in Europe were usually straight but occasionally those of serpentine pattern were built. The severity of line was broken with ornamental posts, sometimes elaborate in design with a decorative cap or a finial, oftentimes an urn or some other sculptured form.

Stone walls were often erected where the material was in good supply. In New England, the stones dug out of the fields were lined up along boundaries in a loose wall. Stone set in cement is of easier construction than a dry wall in which stone is cut and fitted with a precise technique. Whatever type of wall is selected for a garden, it should be remembered that skilled craftsmanship is essential. There are few short cuts to solid construction.

The monotony of bricks and mortar or stone with or without mortar can be relieved with some form of ornament or embellishment to the advantage and completeness of the garden itself. Plant tracery achieved with vines or espaliered trees and shrubs is one solution. Ornamental plaques of various media in metal, terra-cotta, wood, or glazed ceramics offer fascinating possibilities. Wall fountains may be used to advantage. Niches built into walls to provide settings for figures or urns lend pleasing variety. The use of painted treillage or latticework is still another variation. Whatever decorative devices are used need to be selected on the basis of easy and low-cost maintenance.

A serpentine brick wall provides a setting for tropical foliage on two levels. Thomas Jefferson designed one of the earliest of these walls to be built in America on the grounds of the University of Virginia at Charlottesville. *Photo by George Taloumis*

Openwork patterns relieve the monotony and severity of a high cement block wall. The crushed rock in the courtyard contrasts effectively with the smooth surface of the wall, and the large mulberry tree emphasizes the horizontal effect of the site.

Stone walls laid up dry require skill in building to keep them in place. They make pleasing natural boundaries and lend an air of solidarity to a property. When boulders or large stones are available, these make a good foundation. The art of laying is best learned by practice for no amount of telling can accomplish that which results from blistered and bruised hands and aching muscles as well. Much depends on the type of stone available. When rocks abound, what better way to use them than in a wall, freestanding or to hold a bank? Eroded rocks with glacial markings are sometimes uncovered which add interest to the texture and pattern of the wall. *Photos by George Taloumis*

Brick walls designed in the eighteenth century manner with curved brick capping and molded detail are seldom built nowadays. Panels of Chinese design and an Oriental flair in the gate design hark back to an era when Chinoiserie was the rage in garden ornament. A pair of Japanese hollies flank the gate.

A brick and stucco wall becomes an architectural extension of a contemporary house and also provides a stunning background for a desert garden. *Photos by George Taloumis*

A loosely laid stone wall encloses the flower beds in a country garden. *Photo by George Taloumis*

The pineapple, symbol of hospitality, made of terra-cotta—a piece of sculptural collage designed as a wall decoration by John R. Burbidge. *Photos by S. T. Cahill*

A mask carved in pine by a member of the Lang family of Oberammergau, scene of the world-renowned Passion Play. Aging of the wood has given it a rich patina.

A low retaining wall of fieldstone, capped with cement, enhances the pool, the figure, and the paving in this shady terrace planting. *Photos by P. E. Genereux*

A dry wall planted with rock plants; snow-in-summer predominates in June.

Kabuki Players. Sculptural collage—painted terra-cotta mounted on weathered pine boards—by John R. Burbidge. Adapted from a Japanese print portraying a Kabuki drama. *Photo by S. T. Cahill*

10

ORIENTAL GARDEN ORNAMENT

Japanese Garden Ornament

JAPANESE art in its myriad forms reflects the pursuit of perfection. Imbued with a feeling for and an understanding of the enduring quality of beauty, the objects which the Japanese create, as well as the houses they build and the gardens which they design, display a marked feeling of restraint, restfulness, and tranquillity that is beginning to capture the imagination and the sensitive eye of the Westerner. To be sure, the art of pottery making and other highly developed skills, the development of flower arranging and the creation of "nature-inspired" gardens were all derived from China—the fountainhead of Oriental art. Yet, the Japanese have stamped all of their accomplishments in these fields of endeavor with the marks of their own unique culture, since their aesthetic ideals emerged from their own folk culture and island environment. As Mrs. Paul Kincaid has expressed it in *Japanese Garden and Floral Art,* "The Japanese possess the innate artistic sense to assimilate and adapt, absorb and nationalize that which they borrow."

Understatement, illusion, the power of suggestion, subtleness—these are characteristics to be discovered in Japanese art, whether they be displayed in the tea ceremony, the arranging of flowers, or the design of a garden. Zen Buddhism, the source of this aesthetic sense, teaches that the power of suggestion is vital to all the arts because it allows the beholder to complete the concept of what is implied. Every good gardener knows that even with the most careful planning, selecting, and planting, the end result is by no means complete. Growth that requires time and the elements of wind and weather are the forces that shape a garden, together with the attention that is lavished upon it. Yet we seldom ponder or even dwell upon this important aspect of garden philosophy. Every nation through language offers words of subtle and specialized meaning which do not always translate directly. In Japan, the term *shibui* is one of these that implies not only discrimination in taste, but also elegance, simplicity, humility, "serenity, modesty, formality, restraint, and nobility." Blend the sum total of this meaningful word with your concept of a garden and the decoration or ornaments it contains and, if carried out with a sense of order, the result can be astonishing. A reverence for life and for nature as well—the natural order of things—is implied. The resulting serenity achieved derives from "a balance between discipline and freedom." With this brief background, the subtle meaning expressed in the raked gravel surface of a courtyard setting featuring a single camellia of treelike form and several well-placed, moss-covered stones is more easily understood. Texture, form, and the restrained use of color are apparent.

Captivated by Japanese art, numerous attempts have been made throughout America to adapt the principles of Oriental garden making to Western settings. When a garden of this sort is designed around some noteworthy ornament, and an appropriate setting is provided together with suitable plant material, the results often prove most rewarding. The Peabody Museum of Salem, Massachusetts, which contains one of the world's greatest collections of Japanese ethnology has such a garden. The outstanding feature of this garden is a great bronze Japanese temple lantern dating from the eighteenth century. Equally impressive is the syenite boulder, of local origin, weighing more than five tons, which rests at the base of an Oriental crab apple. Rocks are significant elements in all Oriental gardens, for it is believed that no rock however large or small is without some symbolic significance. *Photo, courtesy Peabody Museum*

Copy of an Oriental stoneware flowerpot made in Hong Kong in 1969. Dark blue glaze. Stone mulch. *Photo by S. T. Cahill*

Close-up of Japanese temple lantern on opposite page.

Stone Lanterns

THE stone lantern (*ishi-toro*), one of the conspicuous ornaments in Japanese gardens, has long been a favorite with Western gardeners. These lanterns ranging in height from one to eight feet or more were used for centuries as votive lights in Shinto shrines and Buddhist temples and served also to light the paths leading to the shrines. Later they became a part of nearly every Japanese garden for lighting paths and marking the location of the stone water basin, usually near the entrance to the house. Today, they are considered primarily ornamental. Names of the various styles are derived either from a particular temple or shrine, the place of origin or the person who designed a particular style. The Kasuga lantern, named for a Shinto deity, is particularly imposing both in form and decoration.

Another called the Enshu honors the highest authority on the tea ceremony. The elongated cap with its lotus-bud top suggests the similarly shaped head of Fukurokuju, one of the seven gods of fortune. The snow-scene or snow-viewing lantern (*yukimi-doro*), made of stone or iron, is so called because the wide bowllike top holds the snow. The legs on which it rests are widely spread, producing a striking effect, especially when lighted. Often this type of lantern is placed near a pool, or sometimes on a large rock.

Since the stone lantern symbolizes light dispelling darkness, its placement is important. Nor should it be an isolated ornament. Rather it is most appropriate to plant a small evergreen near it such as a camellia or to so place it that the twisted branches of a pine break across it. A flat stone near the base provides for a place to stand when lighting it. Other accessories in addition to the water basin include symbolic stones for special uses.

A Kasuga stone lantern in a New England garden flanked by a Japanese andromeda (*Pieris japonica*), a widely planted broad-leaved evergreen, and sourwood (*Oxydendrum arboreum*), a summer-flowering tree that is native from Pennsylvania to Florida. Originally small oil lamps or candles were used for illumination in stone lanterns and the light was softened by covering the apertures with translucent paper. Constant exposure to weather gives lanterns an aged appearance, but the antique effect can be induced more rapidly by rubbing the stone surface with buttermilk and keeping it in the shade until the lichen growth develops. Rust color on stone can be created by rubbing a mixture of peanut butter and water into the surface. *Photo by Ronald Rolo*

An unusually large stone snow-scene lantern in Happo-en Garden, Tokyo, rests on a sturdy stone base between two Japanese black pines which lean to frame it. The informal looped-bamboo fence protects the azaleas from intrusion without detracting from the setting. *Photos by George Taloumis*

A stone lantern in the Mitsui Garden in Tokyo. Many of these garden antiques are further embellished with gray, brownish, or green encrustations of lichens. It is believed that the stone lantern originated in Korea, but it has been widely used in Japan for centuries. A cut-leaf maple and a twisted pine together with a mass of ground cover at the base enhance its beauty. The arched footbridge, in the distance, made of wood, is another distinctive feature of the Japanese garden.

An arbor covered with wisteria thoughtfully placed so that its reflection in the water may be enjoyed. The stone snow-scene lantern with its circular base, which rests on a large rock, gives a pleasing balance to this bit of the Orient in the Japanese Garden of the University of Washington at Seattle. *Photo by George Taloumis*

Stones

STONES of every conceivable size and shape, whether brought from a mountainside or the seashore, are an integral part of the Japanese garden. Texture, color, and rarity are also involved in selection, and placement is governed by source of origin as well as shape. In small gardens one may see the "guardian" stone, the "stone of worship," the "stone of two deities," as well as a stone water basin, one or more stone lanterns, stepping-stones, stones used to make a dry stream bed, and smaller stones for ground cover and mulch. In *The World of the Japanese Garden,* Loraine Kuck has written, "A great stone of fine shape and texture was considered a fit gift for a prince." In the year 1229, seventeen oxen were required to move a single stone for the garden of the Gold Pavilion in Kyoto.

Sand

SAND evokes the thought of freshness and cleanness and serves to represent water in a dry landscape. Neatly raked in a variety of patterns to simulate the flow of water, the resulting effect is one of great charm and simplicity. Formalized ripples suggested by wavy lines give a distinctly impressionistic effect to this form of garden art. This kind of simple composition in which sand, rocks, and a minimum of vegetation are used holds strong appeal for builders of contemporary houses. Free-form patterns of moss on sand as seen in several gardens in Kyoto offer a challenge to the imagination of anyone intrigued by a feeling for pattern.

Two clumps of tastefully pruned heavenly bamboo (*Nandina domestica*) add a lacy effect to this entrance planting in Kyoto. The textural effect on the ground includes stone paving, sand for a mulch-like treatment, and tiling at the entrance. The placement of the eroded rocks, the sparse planting showing a variety of foliage forms, and the bamboo rail bespeak restraint and serenity. *Photo by George Taloumis*

The various elements of a Japanese garden are evident in this century-old planting on the grounds of the New Otani Hotel in Tokyo. Superb examples of the Kasuga and snow-scene stone lanterns as well as the stone pagoda among the trees at the right, and the effect created by water, rocks, and vegetation spell out the essence of the Japanese garden to the Western observer.

A skillfully made bamboo fence supported by a low stone wall. The design of the fence, its construction, and the use of heavy cord are details worth observing. *Photos by George Taloumis*

A casually made bamboo fence outlines part of the garden of Sento-Gosho in Kyoto. Encrusted lichens add color and texture to the open-branched tree that frames the entrance. A flowering vine softens one section of the fence and the roof line of the house.

A trimly constructed bamboo fence in Sento-Gosho, Kyoto, offers desired privacy for the grounds of a former emperor's palace. The open gate with its horizontal bamboo pole signifying "private" allows the passerby a glimpse of the garden with its irregularly placed stepping-stones and an ancient Kasuga lantern set amid well-tended shrubs and trees. Even the leaves on the ground reveal the intimate feeling for nature, so meaningful to the Japanese.

This bit of Japanese landscape on the island of Maui, Hawaii, features a wooden lantern near the entrance to a driveway, a neatly made bamboo fence, a great symbolic stone and a pollarded specimen of Australian pine (*Casuarina cunninghamiana*), which lends itself admirably to topiary treatment.

A traditional roofed gate of wood and bamboo at the entrance to a garden filled with azaleas, various ornamental shrubs, and small trees. *Photos by George Taloumis*

Typical of Japanese craftsmanship in construction is the zigzag planked footbridge in Yokohama, built with sturdy posts and beam supports. The simple planting casts shadows for a softening effect. The design suggests the principle that nature abhors a straight line.

Bonsai in porcelain containers arranged on a table for easy viewing in Happo-en Garden, Tokyo.

Mitz Muratami, a Japanese nurseryman in Phoenix, Arizona, has used Swedish myrtle (*Myrtus communis*), native to the Mediterranean region and Western Asia, for a distinctive topiary effect in his garden. The miniature-tree effect created softens the geometric pattern of the lattice and the stone mulch adds materially to the entire effect. Swedish myrtle, an evergreen shrub, three to nine feet high in its native habitat, valued for its small, light green, aromatic foliage, is commonly grown as a tender pot plant except in frost-free areas. *Photo by George Taloumis*

An ancient temple figure from Japan, cut from granite, framed by winged euonymus. *Collection of Allen Haskell; photos by Ronald Rolo*

The crane is deeply rooted in Japanese tradition, symbolizing happiness and longevity because the crane, like the tortoise, is noted for its long lifespan. The pair shown here in hammered metal are excellent examples of craftsmanship in modeling and poise. The large wooden tub bound with iron was used in New Bedford, Massachusetts, in the nineteenth century to hold molasses. *Collection of Allen Haskell*

In the ancient garden of a feudal lord, now part of the grounds of the New-Otani Hotel in Tokyo, we find a stream in which red rocks, rare in this area, are used along the edge and across it, casting their shadow into the clear water. In the foreground, small stones packed in clay make a dramatic textured effect for the stone water basin, a masterpiece of some forgotten stonecutter. *Photo by George Taloumis*

A stone pagoda from Japan, surrounded by ornamental grass and several kinds of bamboo. In Japan, stone pagodas, which may have from three to thirteen or more tiers, are often placed on a hillside in a setting of woody plants or near water where the reflection of the form may be enjoyed. Those with five tiers are especially prized since they represent the four directions of the compass plus the center, also the five elements as known to the Japanese—earth, wood, fire, metal, and water. Originally they were built as memorial or relic towers on the grounds of Buddhist temples, not unlike spires on Christian churches. While symbolizing the supremacy of Buddha and his law which rises above the world and its inhabitants, the pagoda today is primarily a garden ornament. Although many of the old pagodas are monuments to the art of stonecutting, some were made of wood, clay, tile, or bronze. Others were designed as treasure towers with compartments for three, five, or more lights which, when illuminated near pools or streams, produce dramatic lighting effects. *Collection of Allen Haskell; photo by Ronald Rolo*

A small stone pool with spillway creates a miniature stream. The dry stone effect at the left complements the pool, suggesting the feeling of water. Trim evergreen azaleas give a green sculptured effect of pleasing texture resulting in a poetic natural composition. *Photos by George Taloumis*

An ancient water basin cut out of natural stone near the entrance to a shrine in Takamatsu on the island of Shikoku.

Water and stones of various sizes arranged in a natural manner together with ferns, a cut-leaf maple, and azaleas lend notable charm to many Japanese gardens—which are designed with artful skill and simplicity.

In the driveway near the entrance to a house by the sea, a figure of a seated Buddha rests on a block of granite. In his left hand he holds an orangelike fruit, probably either the peach, symbol of longevity, or the fo shou (Buddha's-hand). The latter is a kind of inedible citron, *Citrus medica,* known for its strongly fragrant odor and offered at the New Year Festival and on other occasions before the shrine of the household gods. This fruit connotes Buddhism because its form resembles a classic position of Buddha's hand with the index and little finger pointing upward. It also serves as a symbol of wealth since it signifies the grasping of money. The Buddha's right hand forms a lotus fist, symbolizing the unopened lotus flower, esteemed as an emblem of purity and perfection.

Chinese Garden Seats

Of all the garden ornaments brought from China to the east coast of the United States during the great period of the China Trade (1785–1840), none is more fascinating or more highly prized today than the porcelain garden seats, or barrels as they were called in the shipping lists. Actually, since they were highly restricted in travel, American sea captains saw little or nothing of the residential areas or the great palaces and gardens of China where these seats were in common use. It was only when a favored few were invited to a Hong merchant's house that the "flowery-flag devils," as the Chinese called the Americans, were able to glimpse the Chinese way of life. A comparatively small number of Chinese paintings of gardens and grounds, brought home by sea captains, have survived. These, plus a few brief memoirs, serve as the meager records of what Americans knew about eighteenth and nineteenth century Chinese gardens. Yet hardly a shipment of Chinese porcelain was unloaded in Salem, Boston, Providence, New York, Philadelphia, or other eastern seaboard towns that did not have a few garden seats.

Why the Yankee sea captains were so attracted by these bulky porcelain barrels is not evident. A rundown of items in the early nineteenth century shipping lists reveals that, unlike sets of tableware, porcelain barrels were not brought home in quantity. Perhaps they considered them as novel gifts for wives and sweethearts. Or, as with mantel garniture, they may have been considered as status symbols at the time. In any event, they were notably handsome ornaments for great houses. "India China," as porcelain was known then in both England and America, was indeed a practical luxury. Nearly every piece had some functional use related to everyday life. Unlike the Chinese who had a keen appreciation of beauty in design, the aggressive Yankee traders knew a good salable item when they saw one and were eager to acquire all that they could sell. Garden seats varied from fifteen to twenty inches or more in height and a foot or more in diameter and weighed twelve to twenty pounds apiece. Like the great dinner sets of 172 pieces or more, these barrels with their intricate designs were not only a delight to the eye but impressive in appearance. Unlike dinner or tea sets, they were more decorative than useful. In 1816, William Law of New York purchased two garden seats from the Chinese merchant Manchong for four dollars each. By way of comparison, as to prices then current for chinaware, Benjamin Shreve of Salem purchased a large tea set of 143 pieces "painted in the French manner" for the sum of $30.43. At the time, these expenditures indicated quality merchandise. In the present market, an early nineteenth century garden seat of one of the more common China-trade patterns sells for $400.00 and sometimes considerably more.

The barrel-shaped garden seat or stool is known in China as *liang tun* which means cool seat, an illusion no doubt to a sensation of coolness derived from touching porcelain or from the fact that many extant examples of ancient stools to be found in China were made of stone, the material of which the earliest seats may have been made. Garden seats appear in paintings made during the early part of the Sung dynasty (A.D. 960–1279). They are also found in paintings and drawings of succeeding dynasties and appear in many garden photographs made in the late nineteenth and early twentieth centuries. In practically every set of Chinese paintings depicting the process of porcelain manufacture, the colorful barrels are displayed.

It is claimed that the barrel shape was derived from an ancient Chinese drum of similar form. In addition to the barrel shape, some were made in hexagonal form. Others made of lacquer were definitely square with bulging barrellike sides. Besides porcelain, seats were made of stoneware, wood (both rosewood and lacquer), and brass. Practically all the garden seats imported during the time of the China trade were porcelain seats seen in shops and in private collections. They reveal many kinds of decoration not usually associated with typical export porcelain. These were obviously made for use in China and were exported in the late nineteenth and early twentieth centuries. Some stoneware seats are known to have been brought home by American missionaries. A splendid example of a porcelain seat attributed to the reign of Chien-lung (1736–1796) was described by its owner as follows:

> An unusual Chinese porcelain garden stool of hexagonal form, the top and lower portion is narrower than the main body and having pierced designs. The body is decorated with a continuous landscape design of trees and rocks in which eight horses prance and gallop. The top has a kylin playing with a ball. The whole decoration is in underglaze blue and fleur de peche (It was valued at $1,800.00.)

Those seats decorated in the typical manner of export porcelain are for the most part highly ornate. The overall crowded designs, more Western than Eastern, look more like rug designs than the painting on the seats made for use in China. Famille rose coloring has strong eye appeal and a great number of these of varying quality are to be found in private collections. The dominant motif of famille rose or, more popularly, rose medallion (sometimes spoken of as rose Canton) consists of four panels featuring butterflies, birds, and flowers with a background of rose-colored tree peonies, foliage, and gold. The mandarin pattern is similar in coloring and in motif but with large panels of Chinese figures in landscape settings.

In the nineteenth century, Chinese export porcelain was known as "India China" since it was brought to England and America in ships of the East India Company that stopped at Bombay and Calcutta. It was made of petuntse and kaolin, two types of clay abundant in the region of Ching-tê-chen, the city where these pieces were manufactured. The porcelain was then shipped to the ports of Canton and Nanking where it was exported for Western use.

The blue and white Canton and Nanking porcelains were brought from China in great quantity throughout the entire period of trade. Both patterns are similar in their central design, featuring landscape scenes with bridges, people, boats, islands, trees, notably the willow (which was highly regarded in China), and mountains, but differing in their outer borders. The Canton ware has a dark blue lattice or network border on a solid, light blue background, and wavy or scalloped lines above. The Nanking border has a closer network with each mesh of the net containing a small ornament, and a spearhead, rather than scalloped, border. The traditional story of the irate father chasing his eloping daughter was strictly a legend of English origin. In China, marriages were always arranged by the parents and to these people the depiction of such an idea as elopement would have been preposterous. The original Chinese ware lacked many of the details later supplied by English potters in their copies of Chinese porcelain, referred to as willow ware. The Chinese design elements in the blue and white Canton and Nanking wares were strictly decorative and might vary from set to set. Generally, Nanking ware is of better quality than Canton and was more likely made to order than the Canton china which was often brought over as ballast. As the garden seat was one of the few pieces made in the Chinese form and as these pieces were not brought over in large quantities, it is doubtful that they were made for ballast.

The Fitzhugh pattern in blue and white was less common. The origin of the name of this pattern has long remained a mystery until J. B. S. Holmes tracked down the Fitzhugh family's activities in the British East India Company, which spanned the eighteenth century. It is now believed that the pattern was named in tribute to a member of this family. Consisting of a circular medallion (or occasionally another emblem such as an eagle), surrounded by four panels of floral design, containing pomegranates, symbolic of prosperity, and symbols of Chinese treasures representing the arts, this pattern usually had a wide trelliswork border containing four split pomegranates and butterflies with wings spread. Some Fitzhugh china, probably the earlier type, has the post and spear border usually associated with Nanking china. In other cases, the typical Canton willow-tree motif appeared in the center with a Fitzhugh border. The Fitzhugh pattern was made in other colors than blue and included brown, yellow, green, mulberry, gold, black, and orange. Sometimes a gold outline added further embellishment. A garden seat in Fitzhugh orange recently fetched nearly four thousand dollars.

Celadon, a delicate, sea green color much sought after by connoisseurs, was occasionally used to color the glaze of some of the garden seats. A number of other color variants and combinations, some with subtle variations in shape, were made. The student of Chinese porcelain soon learns to distinguish those pieces commonly made for export from the garden seats believed to have been made specifically for use in China. The latter are less ornate and usually simpler in design as the accompanying photographs reveal.

In the mid-nineteenth century, English porcelain factories, notably Minton and Spode, produced garden seats in quantity. Some of the designs were copies of Chinese export ware while others are more easily identified as English.

Since porcelain garden seats have become collector's items, their value has increased steadily so that it is not feasible to use such valuable articles in most gardens. However, reproductions ranging in price from fifty to one hundred dollars each are available from importers, Oriental shops, and some garden centers.

An English copy (Minton) of Chinese Amoy design is done in blue on white with an overall design of floral scrolls and camellias. The pierced circular intersecting medallions in the center represent Chinese cash or coins and are embellished with lotus scrolls and chrysanthemums. The decorative bands encircling the top and bottom of this piece are filled with cherry blossoms. *Photo by Richard Merrill*

A seat of Fitzhugh design in blue and white has a central motif of two circular intersecting medallions, symbolic of Chinese coins; the medallions and the ribbon which entwines them are decorated with curl-work designs. The central medallion is surrounded by a four-part floral design containing pomegranates, emblem of prosperity, and Chinese treasures, including scrolls and books, celebrating the arts. The spearhead and mesh border is of the Nanking type. Motifs from the central portion are repeated above, enclosed by a wavy band of curl-work. A simpler decoration is depicted at the bottom. The empty white spaces are filled with bosses. The medallion with four surrounding parts is carried out again on the top. *Photos by Richard Merrill*

A Rose Canton specimen has alternating panels of Chinese figures and flowers, birds, butterflies, and bees. A pierced central medallion is seen at the right, and bosses encircle the upper and lower portions. The background is filled with floral scrolls, flowers, leaves, and butterflies. The rose color in this type of porcelain varies from pink to deep purple and is known as the purple of Cassius.

A beautiful large floral medallion is painted on each side of this seat; one depicting tree peonies, the Chinese flower symbol for spring; the other, lotus blossoms for summer. The background is filled with a finely depicted diaper pattern composed of swastikas, an ancient Chinese symbol. The upper portion is embellished with bosses, floral scrolls and blossoms, and a border of the key or meander pattern. Other decorative motifs fill the lower portion. The Chinese did not like empty spaces, hence they filled in backgrounds and borders with many of these diaper patterns. *Photos by Richard Merrill*

A Chinese landscape design enhances the main portion of this Nanking example. Further embellishment is provided by the wavy floral bands decorated with cherry blossoms and bosses on the upper and lower portions of this piece. The upper border contains Chinese treasure symbols entwined with ribbons. The Chinese did not consider a piece of art complete unless it had a border.

Chinese figures in a landscape setting occupy a large central medallion. The background design is a diaper pattern with swastika motif. Bands containing bosses, cherry blossoms, mesh devices, and small panels of flowers encircle the top. Other decorative motifs used to fill space cover the bottom portion of the seat. The pierced cash symbol, diaper pattern, and floral panels are repeated on the top. *Photo by Richard Merrill*

A hexagonal stoneware garden seat made in China in the early nineteenth century. The six reticulated floral panels are glazed in dark blue, green, yellow, and straw color. Unlike the porcelain garden seats in the Fitzhugh, Canton, rose medallion and mandarin patterns made for export, this type was more commonly used in Chinese gardens.

As with sculpture, ornamental urns of various kinds have a place in gardens where there is ample space to enjoy their beauty of form. This Chinese bronze urn designed in the traditional style of the Chou dynasty is believed to have been made for the European market in the eighteenth century when the rage for Chinoiserie was at its height. The rings for carrying it are held by glutton masks (tao'tieh). Large yellow, white, and bronzy orange chrysanthemums applied in cloisonné highlight the surface. *Photos by S. T. Cahill*

Porcelain flowerpots, jardinieres, and fishbowls as made in China, especially those produced for domestic use, were decorated in traditional Chinese taste with figures of animals, birds, and flowers composed with a vivid sense of symbolism. In their decoration they are in a class apart from the porcelains produced for the American and European markets with their busy, somewhat crowded patterns. Many of the large deep bowls that are usually referred to as jardinieres were more commonly used as fishbowls in China. Often they were placed on pedestals in the courtyard or near the house where the owner might enjoy watching his fish swimming about. The blue and white container holds a lacecap hydrangea; the famille rose, a sasanqua camellia. *Photos by S. T. Cahill*

Canton porcelain fishbowl decorated in blue and white. *Photo courtesy The Peabody Museum*

Two hexagonal stoneware plant stands or pedestals of nineteenth century Chinese origin brought to America during the days of the China Trade. The glaze colors throughout are similar to those of the garden seat. The openwork designs in the panels, like those found in Chinese wall tiles, add materially to the decorative effect of these sturdy pieces of furniture. They were used to display favorite potted plants in halls, living rooms, and on verandahs in Chinese houses. *Photos by S. T. Cahill*

Among the curios brought home by sea captains engaged in the China Trade in the nineteenth century were earthenware elephants. Like the porcelain garden seats they could be used as stools or as stands to hold potted plants. In recent years they have been reproduced and shipments from Hong Kong are often displayed in specialty shops. *Photo by George Taloumis*

A stoneware garden seat of unusual design and coloring, brought to America by a missionary in the late nineteenth century. Garden seats make useful small tables for terraces and elsewhere in the garden. Reproductions, often found in solid colors, with a minimum of decoration, are available at modest cost. The slaty-metallic glaze is washed with sang de boeuf.

Reproductions of Oriental flowerpots make highly decorative containers. This example in stoneware finished in dark blue glaze holds a Swiss stone pine pruned and shaped to become a miniature tree.

Six tiles in green glaze, made in Hong Kong, enclosed in a wooden frame for use as an openwork panel in a garden wall or a gate. These tiles, copied from old Chinese designs, are available in several sizes. *Photos by S. T. Cahill*

This handsome porcelain garden seat is an unusual specimen of hexagonal form with pierced decorations in the upper and lower portions. A landscape design on the body, executed in the traditional Chinese manner of portraying nature, depicts eight horses prancing among trees and rocks. The eight horses of Mu Wang, fifth sovereign of the Chou dynasty, are renowned in Chinese legends and are often used as an art motif. The border is the key, or meander pattern. On the top is a kylin playing with a ball. The colors are underglaze blue and fleur de peche. This seat is of much finer quality in craftsmanship and decoration than the typical barrels produced for export and undoubtedly was made for use in China. *Photo by Edward Garratt*

Porcelain flowerpots, used in China for centuries, were shipped to America occasionally but were never common. This hexagonal pot, measuring 11¾ inches wide and 9½ high, complete with saucer, is believed to have been made in the early nineteenth century. The rose medallion decoration featuring Chinese figures in landscape settings is of superior quality. *Photos by S. T. Cahill*

Flagstone set in sand makes an inviting walk through an allée of willows that leads to the sea. Ferns and pachysandra serve as underplanting and ground cover. *Photo by McFarland*

11

WALKS AND PATHS

WELL-DESIGNED walks and paths are essential elements of garden design since they provide the means for circulation. Solid surfaces, adequate drainage, trim edges, and a feeling of spaciousness are basic requirements for use, comfort, maintenance, and eye appeal. A walk or a path needs to be inviting, since it spells out a note of welcome and reflects the hospitality of the owner. It needs to be safe for use in all weather. A nonskid surface is one approach to safety linked with provision for drainage.

All too many garden walks are planned on the narrow side. Since two people should be able to walk abreast with ease, a minimum of four feet width is essential and a five-foot walk is even more desirable. Because walks and paths are needed for access, the approach should be direct. A straight line is the shortest distance between two points. Avoid the use of curved walks unless they fit the site. The use of meandering curves is dictated by the terrain as when a tree, a group of shrubs, a ledge, or a large rock suggests the need for a curve.

Grass paths are pleasing to the eye and easy to tread upon, but constant use, particularly in a small garden, requires frequent resodding. (Reseeding is much too slow a process.) Where needed, grass makes an ideal surface for secondary walks. These need to be planned for easy mowing and edging. Better still, a permanent edging of brick, stone, or metal is the solution to reduced maintenance.

Where natural effects are sought, chopped bark (commonly used for mulching) spread to a depth of two to three inches over a well-drained surface makes an ideal walk. Tanbark and pine needles, when obtainable, serve the same purpose. All of these materials need renewing every two to three years. The use of a well-packed, heavy layer of chopped bark, tanbark, or pine needles involves little expense and adds greatly to the appearance of a natural landscape. Furthermore, their color and texture leaves little to be desired. Planting, which often flanks this type of walk, needs to be controlled, especially when ground-cover plants are involved.

Washed gravel (referred to as peastone or roofer's gravel) is commonly used. It allows for quick drainage after a rain, makes a pleasing color and textural effect and tends to pack with constant use. The initial layer of gravel may need to be tamped or rolled to produce a firm foundation. Too loose a surface makes walking difficult, especially when openwork shoes or sandals are worn.

Crushed stone of fine texture, derived from sandstone, marble, bluestone, or limestone is sometimes used for garden walks, especially where specific color effects are sought. Successful use and desired effects are contingent on the site and the play of light and shadow. In bright sunlight, light-colored, especially white, walks can be blinding in their effect. Careful attention to the foundation prepared for crushed stone aids in settling the surface.

Paving with blocks or rounds of wood is sometimes used where wood is in plentiful supply, but maintenance is a constant requirement. Treating the wood surfaces with a preservative and firm placement assure longer use.

Brick and stone, laid with an eye to design, add pattern, texture, and color to the overall effect. Water-struck brick is the only kind to use since ordinary building brick soon deteriorates due to frost and weather. Patterns used in laying bricks may be simple or intricate according to the desire of the designer. In gardens where foliage effects predominate over flower color, patterned brick walks are often featured to good advantage.

As with brick, flagstone and bluestone, whether cut or laid in a random pattern, may be set in sand or cement. In either case, a well-prepared foundation is essential.

Concrete and asphalt, in common use because of the moderate cost involved, offer the least in eye appeal, but they are permanent surfaces for all seasons and when properly laid with well-prepared foundations require a minimum of maintenance. Lampblack added to cement helps to darken the natural color and make it less glaring in the sunlight.

Stepping-stones, of sufficient size and smooth surface, when carefully set, have a place in gardens where traffic is light and the time required for maintenance is not a factor. Grass surrounding them needs constant trimming. Spacing is important to accommodate the length of stride for those using the path. Otherwise, a ragged, irregular streak results, due to the wear on the grass surrounding the stones.

Bluestone is an ideal material for paving a terrace. When change of level occurs and sturdy walls are required, granite set in cement makes a harmonious combination, especially when lampblack is used in the cement mix to darken the seams. Azaleas, some in terra-rosa and others in clay pots, link one level with the other. *Photo by Ronald Rolo*

A border of shells and washed gravel makes a decorative edging for an old brick wall beside a bed of periwinkle in the Alexander Craig garden in Williamsburg, Virginia. *Courtesy, Colonial Williamsburg*

Stepping-stones gathered from the nearby stony terrain and some excavated when the place was planted emphasize the color and texture of the ancient stone wall that surrounds this enchanting spring garden. *Photo by Paul E. Genereux*

Peastone or washed gravel used for a walk in an old boxwood-bordered garden complements the silvery gray edging of artemisia Silver Mound used in the adjoining flower beds. *Photo by Walton T. Crocker*

A neatly laid brick walk set in sand and brick steps with easy risers are an integral part of a well-tailored landscape effect. *Photo by George Taloumis*

A spacious walk made of Belgian block has the added value of permanence. Bluestone was used for the treads of the steps. *Photo by Ronald Rolo*

Driveway paving is usually handled with a minimum of imagination. Concrete slabs and a strip of grass laid with an eye to pattern add interest to this service area. *Photo by George Taloumis*

Trimly cut bluestone makes a practical and attractive surface for a terrace that doubles as an approach to a small house. Similar use of bluestone to edge the flower beds adds materially to the effect. An attractive lantern of good scale, a small figure of St. Francis, and a handsome clematis are ornamental features that enhance the setting. *Photo by Paul E. Genereux*

Irregular granite slabs, generous in size, placed random fashion, lead to an enclosed garden. *Photo by Ronald Rolo*

Railroad ties make easy-to-use risers for garden steps and tie in with the natural planting. *Photo by McFarland*

The color and texture of an old brick walk accentuate the richness of the various greens in the adjoining evergreen plantings. The result is year-round eye appeal. *Photos by George Taloumis*

Change of level in a seaside garden has been achieved with the use of cut-granite steps softened with thyme and sedum.

The interplay of horizontal and vertical lines in this contemporary outdoor living area designed by Ned Rucker is echoed in the parquet effect of the planking on a prefab redwood deck. *Photo by Phil Palmer. Courtesy, California Redwood Association*

The value of redwood deck as an extension of the home is illustrated in this use of a deck built on a steep canyonside lot. Here the permanent decking, installed on two levels, turns a lost bit of yard space into a quiet garden area. Note the matching of the deck to the brick pattern. Design by Royston, Hanamoto and Mayes. *Photo by Ken Molino*

In a mild climate, a well-designed redwood deck can be used to create an outdoor living area on a hilly site at the fraction of the cost of adding an inside room. Designed by Katy and Paul Steinmetz.

Belgian block (cut granite) skillfully laid in an effective pattern adds greatly to the appearance of the large forecourt of a Williamsburg-style residence that also serves as a driveway.

Pieces of chipped stone imbedded in concrete make patterned steps in the Mitsui Garden, Tokyo, which lead to a shrub garden where the large flat stepping-stones are imbedded in pebbles to create the effect of walking across a streambed. *Photos by George Taloumis*

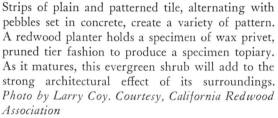

Strips of plain and patterned tile, alternating with pebbles set in concrete, create a variety of pattern. A redwood planter holds a specimen of wax privet, pruned tier fashion to produce a specimen topiary. As it matures, this evergreen shrub will add to the strong architectural effect of its surroundings. *Photo by Larry Coy. Courtesy, California Redwood Association*

A combination of brick, stone, and tile, all set in concrete, provides variety in the texture and pattern of the paving. The radial pattern of the flooring accentuates the linear effect sought in this contemporary setting. The vertical lines of the two large containers, repeated in the fence design, give a feeling of spaciousness. *Photo by Larry Coy. Courtesy, California Redwood Association*

Flagstone paving laid in a random pattern makes a most appropriate surface for a terrace. Grass acts as a filler between the flagstones, requiring more maintenance than concrete seams, but providing a pleasant contrast to the hard, cold surface of the stone. The use of varied sizes of stone arranged in a pleasing pattern lends a charming air of informality to the setting. *Photo by Paul E. Genereux*

A terrace made of rectangular concrete slabs complements the clean lines of a contemporary house. The rough texture of the paving, made by pressing pebbles into wet concrete, provides a pleasing contrast to the smooth walls of the building. Rough surfaces are safer to walk on in wet weather. *Photos by Paul E. Genereux*

Brick laid tight in the basket-weave pattern makes an ideal walking surface for all seasons and accentuates the trim boxwood edging of the flower beds. The substantial wall at the right is built of cut granite. *Photo by George Taloumis*

12

TOPIARY AND PLANTS AS ORNAMENTS

Topiary

CNIUS MARTIUS, reputed to have been a friend of the Emperor Augustus, is believed to have been the first "tree barber" concerned with what we know as the art of topiary. Definitions and reactions to this curious skill of creating "verdant sculpture" remain today, as in the past, conspicuously pointed in their perspective. The training of shrubs and trees into ornamental or grotesque shapes (depending upon individual taste and reaction) is a simple definition for the term topiary. "Tippiery," "Tipperary," "topary trees" and "Eutopia" are some of the "malaprops" that have arisen.

In Roman times, the topiarius or hedge trimmer, even as a slave, was a craftsman of no mean skill, employed to care for the hedges and mazes in the gardens of Cicero and his contemporaries. Pliny referred to clipped hedges and topiary frequently in his writings.

For many centuries, topiary flourished in Europe with spirited revivals at intervals until the beginning of the eighteenth century when a trend toward landscape gardening obliterated much of the formalism that had been popular. In 1736, Thomas Hancock, who owned an impressive house and garden on Boston's Beacon Hill wrote to England for "100 Small Yew Trees in the Rough, which I'd Frame up here to my own Fancy." Aside from gardens linked with historic houses and settings such as Colonial Williamsburg, present-day enthusiasm is somewhat limited. The Hunnewell garden in Wellesley, Massachusetts, became famous for its topiary collection in the mid-nineteenth century and was frequently pictured in garden books. Its owner was an accomplished patron of horticulture and, under the care of his skilled gardeners, this estate became one of the most elaborate examples of topiary art in America.

An English garden that has been as widely photographed as it has been visited in the last two decades is Hidcote Manor in Gloucestershire. It was designed after the turn of the present century by Major Lawrence Johnston, an American who settled in England, and is noted for its extraordinary collection of woody plants. Among them are superb examples of topiary including pairs of peacocks fashioned in yew placed for accent in various rooms of this great garden. The neatly clipped hedges that adjoin them and serve to divide the plantings blend harmoniously with the green sculptured birds.

In a sense some of the topiary one sees today may be described as folk art rather than fine art, especially when there is little rhyme or reason as to its placement or its sculptured effect. The current trend in suburbia of clipping shrubs tightly, both flowering kinds and evergreens, into dull and unimaginative geometric shapes is a prime example of a poor and meaningless attempt at topiary. On the other hand, when it is executed with skill and fits the setting as embellishment or to excite interest, topiary has strong appeal.

In contrast to the typical method of creating topiary art, in which shrubs and trees are shaped with shears, is the practice of training plants on wire frames, sometimes filled with sphagnum moss. This phase of container gardening is currently enjoying a revival of interest. Varieties of English ivy, particularly the small-leaved kinds of the free-branching Pittsburgh ivy, are especially favored. Dainty leaf patterns, some variegated and others curled, produce pleasing-textured form when so grown. Climbing or creeping fig (*Ficus pumila*) and the small-leaved form of euonymus (*Euonymus fortunei minimus*) are also used.

Wire frames in an extensive variety of forms including traditional geometric objects like globes, cones, and columns, as well as animals and birds such as rabbits, does, lambs, turtles, roosters, eagles, dogs, cats, seals, cranes, peacocks, geese, and the like are obtainable from dealers or they are made to specifications by ingenious amateurs. Most of these which are scaled to fit containers are similar to the larger frames used by gardeners to guide them in shaping shrubs with shears.

Two methods of growing "green sculpture" are in common use. Some gardeners prefer to start plants in containers and train them by tying the trailing growth to welded steel wire frames which have been anchored securely in the containers before the plants are set. Others stuff frames covered with chicken wire, using moist, long-grained sphagnum moss which has been moistened with water containing liquid fertilizer. Rooted cuttings are planted in the moss on all sides of the frame, so dispersed as to make possible fairly even foliage growth. In addition, one or more plants are usually set in soil at the base of the frame. After planting, the frame is sprinkled thoroughly and kept in a shaded location for several days until the roots are established in the moss. Daily watering of the mossed frame is essential and liquid fertilizer is added to the water and applied once a month. Young well-rooted cuttings are preferable to old woody-stemmed vines. Shaping is improved by using metal hairpins to keep the new growth in place. Varieties of Pittsburgh ivy as well as the creeping fig are not hardy and must be kept indoors in winter, preferably in a cool temperature.

An outstanding example of garden sculpture in topiary made of variegated English ivy growing in a footed wooden container. Stone mulch helps to retain soil moisture. *Photo by Hampfler Studio*

The vogue for geometry in eighteenth century European gardens was transplanted to America by the few who could afford such luxury. Among them was William Tryon, royal governor of North Carolina. When his palace and gardens were restored (1952–1959), a formal green garden was planted with dwarf yaupon (an evergreen holly native in the South) and trimmed with great precision, as were the trees used for accent and the surrounding hedges. A limestone statue *Boy with Grapes,* has been used as the central feature of this elaborate parterre.

Boy with Grapes
Photos by Herbert Rea. Courtesy, Tryon Palace Restoration

Barnyard fowl modeled in wire serve as a frame which is stuffed with sphagnum moss to make ivy topiary. The Italian terra-cotta pots, in the basket weave pattern, make ideal containers for these green birds. The more frequently new growth is pinned into place, the more distinct the form.

This partially developed eagle trained as ivy topiary reveals the wire structure filled with sphagnum moss. *Photo by George Taloumis*

The Palace Garden. Formal gardens when viewed from a distance so that the overall design can be appreciated amaze and delight the eye. Color, form, and texture in the various segments are happily related in these beds at Colonial Williamsburg. Plant materials and patterns are similar to those used two hundred years ago. *Courtesy, Colonial Williamsburg*

Formal treatment of a small area is effectively executed in the King's Arms Garden at Colonial Williamsburg. Small rectangular plots are accented in each corner with holly topiary in the eighteenth century manner. Brick walls and white picket fencing frame the patterned effect. *Courtesy, Colonial Williamburg*

With a painted open board fence to protect it, this apple tree is a fitting and handsome ornament at every season of the year and helps to tie the house in with its rural setting. *Photo by George Taloumis*

An apple tree trained as an espalier using the double cordon pattern offers a leafy tracery against the weathered-shingle wall of a small house. The art of pruning espaliered fruit requires considerable skill and judgment, but the results are more gratifying, not so much in the amount of fruit produced as in the highly ornamental effect achieved. *Photos by George Taloumis*

The harshness of a light-colored concrete wall is softened and enhanced by two large fire thorns trained as espaliers against it. Both the tracery of the branches and the shadows which they cast, as well as the refined foliage and showy reddish berries, create a highly decorative effect along the driveway of a Reno, Nevada, residence.

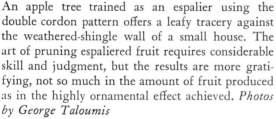

Growing choice fruit espalier fashion with a trellis support was a favorite method in Europe for centuries. This planting of peaches at Colonial Williamsburg suggests a practice which the colonists in eighteenth century America enjoyed. The sturdy brick wall affords protection as well as a setting for the fruit trees. Pears, apples, plums, and quinces also are trained in this manner. Espaliers offer year-round eye appeal, whether it be twig pattern in winter, flower tracery in spring, or foliage and fruit effect in summer.

Large wall surfaces without windows lend themselves to the espaliering of shrubs and trees or the use of clinging vines. Maintenance is greatly reduced when the right tree is chosen as with the cedar of Lebanon used here as a freestanding espalier. The characteristic growth habit gives the effect of tracery which is further enhanced with the play of light and shadow. *Photo by Ronald Rolo*

Exfoliating bark is one of Nature's ways of providing additional ornament in the winter landscape. Korean stewartia, a summer-flowering tree, bears single white camellialike flowers followed by vermillion foliage in autumn. This specimen has flourished at the end of a driveway in a New England garden for more than forty years. Mature trees are notably decorative since the varicolored bark flakes irregularly revealing the lighter color and smooth texture of an inner layer. The sycamore, the paper birch, the lacebark pine, and the crape myrtle are the other woody plants noted for this curious habit of flaking. *Photos by George Taloumis*

Spaced pickets topped with latticework provide desired privacy as well as a suitable background for English ivy trained in a formal manner.

The surface of the weathered redwood walls of a contemporary house is softened with an espaliered Atlas cedar (*Cedrus atlantica*). This ancient tree with its blue green, needlelike foliage, one of several species described by E. H. Wilson, the noted plant hunter, "as surviving remnants of prehistoric forests of enormous magnitude," is highly valued for its longevity and the texture of its foliage. Careful pruning will help to keep it in scale with its surroundings. The mulch of beach stones is both practical and attractive.

Evergreen espalier effects are possible with the adaptable Japanese yew. Hicks, Hatfield, and other upright forms of this dependable evergreen (especially those plants allowed to grow naturally in the nursery without the benefit of heavy pruning which makes the stems less tractable) lend themselves to training in this fashion. If a more open tracery effect is desired, cutting out undesirable growth is the answer. Where more rigid or formal patterns are suitable, these can be created in the same way.

Pots of agapanthus, the blue lily of the Nile, rate high as garden ornaments. When they are in prime flowering condition (potbound), the clusters of blue tubular flowers on two- to four-foot stems flaunt their beauty for a month or more in midsummer. At all seasons the straplike foliage lends an architectural effect to the garden. In cold climates, these tender tuberous-rooted plants need frost-free storage over winter. *Photo by Walton T. Crocker*

In a sense the art of pruning, shaping, and training plants may be compared to the art of sculpting. When plants are trained as espaliers, they can be adapted to fit a site as illustrated and become prime elements of decoration. Espaliered geraniums are by no means common since it requires several years to develop sizable specimens. In cold climates they are stored in a plant room or greenhouse over winter. *Photos by George Taloumis*

Line, form, and texture are brought into play with a high hedge that flanks a gate of contemporary design. In marked contrast, the Oriental feeling of the foreground planting of Pfitzer junipers, pruned and shaped to suggest large bonsai, complements the gate design.

When placed in the right site, yucca or Adam's needle, as it is sometimes called, becomes a noteworthy plant ornament. Both the flowers and the seedpods are highly decorative as structural accents, and the foliage is equally impressive in form, line, and texture.

Usually these broad-leaved evergreens develop into large, roundheaded, symmetrical specimens when grown in the open. However, with the skillful use of the pruning shears, picturesque forms can be maintained over a long period of years to serve as evergreen sculptured ornament.

Wisteria develops heavy woody stems as it matures and takes on a gnarled picturesque appearance, provided the pruning hook and a pair of sharp shears are kept in use constantly. This practice induces more flower buds as well. Left to itself, the entwining tendrils tend to produce an untidy mass of growth which soon reaches into nearby trees. If you would have a noteworthy wisteria, Oriental in aspect, shape it, control it and prune it as is done in its native home—the Orient.

The compactly designed pattern of the garden of the Powell-Waller House in Williamsburg, Virginia, is more fully appreciated when seen from above. Extensive use of box and holly sets off the color provided by tulips and flowering dogwood. Cherokee roses cover the fence in the foreground. *Courtesy, Colonial Williamsburg*

The wind, the storms, the salt spray, and occasionally the hand of a skilled pruner keep this red pine pleasingly horizontal in a Japanese garden near the sea in Rhode Island. *Photo by George Taloumis*

Wind Sculpture

WITHIN reach of the sea, plants frequently assume curious and picturesque forms, contorted by the prevailing winds. Nature with all the force of her power holds dominant sway, often using wind pruning and salt spray to sculpt trees and shrubs in the most elemental of art forms, stripping ruthlessly leaf and flower, twig and branch.

Ernest H. Wilson, the most extraordinary plant hunter of the twentieth century, has described the great struggle of the forces of nature vividly in *Aristocrats of the Trees*. In a chapter entitled "Trees and the Heart of Man," he wrote: "The Monterey Cypress and other coastwise trees may be dubbed Coastguards, defenders of their rockbound homes. Wind is their great enemy and the feud between them is eternal. From youth to old age the struggle persists and marvelous is the fight the trees of the shore put up against their unrelenting, death-dealing enemy, wind. The struggle may go on through centuries yet sooner or later victory is with the wind, but nothing in the tree world commands admiration more than the magnificent fight an Old Pine or Cypress puts up. . . . One can imagine the jaws firmly set, every fiber of the tree's existence stressed to hold its own and proudly floating from the treetop its flag inscribed *nil desperandum*. There is something sublime in the masterful struggle between the organic and inorganic forces and methinks old Mother Nature stands as umpire witnessing the noble game."

On slopes and banks and flat surfaces as well, the various low-growing junipers that thrive in full sun produce richly textured effects which are notably ornamental. This wavy carpet of blue green and silvery gray (*Juniperus horizontalis* Blue Wave) contrasts effectively with the mass of dwarf rhododendrons that surround the granite birdbath. *Photo by Ronald Rolo*

Plants as Ornaments

ART forms in nature are evident everywhere one looks—in woodland, field, pasture, and garden. Geometric precision may be seen in leaf patterns, the silhouettes of evergreens, the bare limbs of trees, and the structural lines of herbaceous plants. The lens of a camera makes us all the more aware of the marvelous symmetry of these forms. Thus, plants often provide the gardener with unique ornaments that are highly decorative in form, texture, and color. The accomplished gardener, aware of this source of nature's bounty, tends to sculpt nature to preserve and maintain the beauty of the plants he cultivates. The elements—wind, weather, snow, ice, and the varying intensities of light—are the forces he contends with in achieving his goal.

Wind and weather add to nature's artistry by lopping off a branch, or twisting a tree trunk or dwarfing natural upright growth, thus creating picturesque forms distinctive for their asymmetrical beauty. These occurrences in the wild or in a garden offer a challenge to the gardener who, by selective pruning, may be able to further enhance and define a unique kind of beauty in form and line.

Soft heavy snow and ice have a way of destroying the natural symmetry of woody plants, and it often takes more than ordinary skill to prune and reshape damaged specimens, but it is usually worth the effort. Frequently, it takes several years for a tree or shrub to recover. Selective pruning at intervals may be required to restore the typical habit of growth or to induce a new shape.

Light is still another factor that influences growth. New shoots reach for the strongest source of light, often creating a pattern of growth which, though not characteristic, has notable eye appeal. This condition often results when plants are placed near the walls of buildings, against a fence, a ledge, or a garden wall. Again, the skillful use of pruning shears results in a plant form that is highly ornamental.

Like sculpture, these living ornaments require a setting if they are to be enjoyed and enough space for controlled development. Invasive growth behind or near them must be kept in check. Even more important is the need to select suitable sites for shrubs and trees of distinctive habit so that the garden may evolve as a setting for them. Frequently we speak of them as accent plants since they possess eye-catching appeal. As with well-placed sculpture, plants of distinctive habit, grown and shaped with an eye to form, are a prime source of garden embellishment. They are nature's choicest ornaments.

13

WEATHER VANES

WEATHER VANES were supposedly invented by the Greeks and the device was later used by the Romans. The most renowned of the early vanes was a triton, still standing, on top of the Tower of the Winds, built by Andronicus, circa 48 B.C. Thomas Jefferson was undoubtedly influenced in his choice of a weather vane for Monticello by an account of an ancient writer on agriculture and architecture, one Marcus Terentius Varro.

Early American weather vanes were first imported or based on European designs. Before long, craftsmen began to develop new interpretations of old forms, and the weather vane soon became a folk art form of the highest order. The earliest vanes were simple ones, made of flat sheet metal or wood. In the latter part of the eighteenth century, craftsmen began to experiment with a more lifelike, three-dimensional form. Early molds for these were made of wood. Early in the nineteenth century, cast-iron molds were developed, from which full-bodied copper weather vanes could be produced. By the end of the century scientific weather prediction and aviation made use of the weather vane in a more technical sense. Many weather vanes, still standing in their original positions after two hundred or more years, are widely admired today for their beauty as well as their usefulness.

Over the centuries, weather vanes have assumed many forms: of all the birds, the cock and the eagle are the most popular; all sorts of animals have been portrayed, both domestic and wild. First and foremost among these is the horse—many images of famous racehorses were produced commercially in the latter part of the nineteenth century. Cows were a popular choice for barns, and country estates often sported deer and dogs. An interest in heraldic devices, popular in medieval Europe, was revived by Sir Christopher Wren who considered the weather vane an important architectural detail. He designed many handsome vanes in the form of medieval banners. The Gothic revival in architecture in the nineteenth century led to further adaptation of banners, arrows, and other heraldic devices.

Geographical location was a determining factor in the design of weather vanes—along the seacoast one saw ships, many carved of wood and gaily painted, and fish. Whales could be found in ports such as Nantucket and New Bedford. Occupations and hobbies of owners were a factor also, and business establishments often advertised their products via weather vanes. Figure types such as Indians, angels, and romantic nineteenth century adaptations of classical prototypes, such as the goddess of liberty, had their heyday.

The most famous of all weather vane craftsmen was Shem Drowne, a Boston coppersmith. His best-known work is the full-bodied grasshopper, made of copper kettles in 1742, that still adorns Faneuil Hall in Boston's market area. It is said that Drowne, as a young boy, was chasing a grasshopper along the banks of the Charles River, when he befriended Peter Faneuil. The Drowne family took the young man in and gave him his start in business. In later years when he became a wealthy merchant, Faneuil commissioned Drowne to make the giant weather vane in the form of a grasshopper to commemorate their meeting.

Another remarkable mid-eighteenth century New England weather vane was the *Flying Mercury*. Nearly five feet tall, carved of wood and gaily painted, it perched on a cupola atop the octagonal domed summerhouse of Colonel Isaac Royall in Medford, Massachusetts.

Some weather vanes were interesting, not only for their artistry, but also for their place or point of view in history. Such a vane was the one designed for George Washington's mansion at Mount Vernon. After the Revolution he had a deep desire for peace and his choice of a dove reflects his personal feelings.

Related to the weather vane as a device powered by the wind is the whirligig—a kind of wind toy or windmill. A whimsical product of the whittler's art, this type of indicator was found, at times, in nineteenth century gardens, perhaps placed there to amuse children.

The art of making weather vanes continues to this day. Full-bodied copper weather vanes are still handcrafted by two of the oldest firms in that business: J. W. Fiske, Inc., of Paterson, New Jersey, and F. G. Washburne Company of Danvers, Massachusetts.

Full-bodied peacock weather vanes of hammered copper finished in gold leaf are by no means common. *Photo by Ronald Rolo*

The finishing touch to the mansion at Mount Vernon, a weather vane in the form of a dove of peace, was added to the cupola in autumn of 1787. Washington wanted the bird to be symbolic as well as useful, and specified: "I should like to have a bird . . . with an olive branch in its mouth. The bird need not be large (for I do not expect that it will traverse with the wind and therefore may receive the real shape of a bird, with spread wings)." Ken Fitzgerald, author of *Weathervanes and Whirligigs,* considered this a very personal weather vane, expressing Washington's hope for peace. *Photo, courtesy Mount Vernon Ladies' Association*

A full rigged clipper ship, its sails billowing in the wind, makes an impressive full-bodied weather vane. Vessels such as this have been popular wind indicators in New England seacoast towns since the nineteenth century when they were first made commercially. All types of sailing ships have been depicted, some made as models of a particular vessel. The earliest examples were made of wood, or a combination of wood and metal. Later ships were made of copper, then of less expensive aluminum. *Photo, E. G. Washburne & Company*

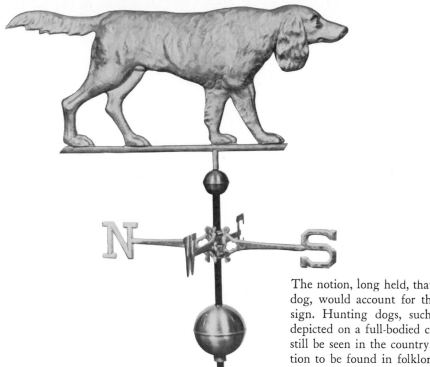

The notion, long held, that man's best friend is his dog, would account for the popularity of this design. Hunting dogs, such as this English setter depicted on a full-bodied copper weather vane, can still be seen in the country. There is also a connection to be found in folklore between dogs and the weather; consider such expressions as "dog days" and "raining cats and dogs." Dogs have been used also as symbols of the wind; a small vane located on the windward rail of a boat is called a "dogvane." *Photo by William Charles. Courtesy, E. G. Washburne & Company*

Cows can be found on the roofs of many a dairy barn and silo. As farming became more specialized, commercial weather vane manufacturers increased their production of livestock animals. By the end of the nineteenth century, various breeds of cows were depicted. Sometimes these animals were painted by dairy farmers to show the colors of their breed; these became very decorative pieces. Present-day craftsmen continue to make copper weather vanes such as this one from old molds. *Photo by Ken Witham. Courtesy, E. G. Washburne & Company*

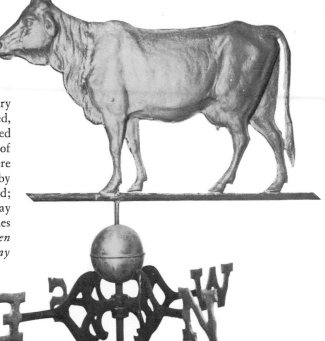

Horse weather vanes, such as this well-bodied copper model of racehorse Ethan Allen, have been produced in America since 1865. Many famous racehorses have been immortalized in this manner. Oftentimes, farmers and stable owners were inspired to try their hand at the art, producing outstanding images of their favorite animals. Today, horse weather vanes, such as this one made from an old mold, continue to be among the best sellers, according to craftsmen who specialize in this business. *Courtesy, E. G. Washburne & Company*

The cock rates as one of the oldest weather-vane subjects, having been in use since the ninth century when a papal decree required that a rooster be placed on the top of every church as a reminder of the betrayal of Christ and as a call to prayer. This bird continued to be a popular symbol for centuries and reached its peak as a design element from the seventeenth to the nineteenth century. In America, early models were made of wood or tin. Gradually, the earlier stylized religious symbols gave way to greater realism and different strains of poultry were displayed on New England meetinghouses and elsewhere. Later, full-bodied copper models were made, and during the late nineteenth and twentieth centuries, weather-vane manufacturers capitalized on the interest of poultry raising for cockfighting and exhibition at country fairs. Shown here are two examples of weather vanes still being made from old molds. *Courtesy, E. G. Washburne & Company*

An amusing piece of contemporary folk art is this wooden weather vane, suggestive of carving done in the early nineteenth century along the New England coast, when wood was plentiful and farmers and fishermen spent their winter evenings whittling. *Photo by Ronald Rolo*

14

WATER IN THE GARDEN

THE earliest source of water in the garden was the well. In ancient times the well was the social center of the community and its importance led to its embellishment. In medieval times the wellhead and conduit head were often elaborately decorated.

During the Renaissance, water was foremost in the layout of the villa garden. Rivers were diverted for water supply, and the art of fountain construction reached its height.

Fountains and other water ornaments were used in a lavish manner in seventeenth century French gardens; trick or joke fountains were popular on the Continent and also in England. In return for his curiosity, an innocent visitor to a garden of that period might be rewarded with a good soaking. One of the earliest English examples of a trick fountain was found at Nonesuch Place, a hunting lodge built for King Henry VIII in Surrey. A trick fountain, one of several in the Renaissance garden at Wilton House, Wiltshire, laid out in 1632, was described as having "many fine figures of ye goddesses, and about 2 yards off the doore is several pipes in a line that with a sluce spouths water up to wett the strangers." A trick willow-tree fountain at Chatsworth, made in 1829 and thought to be a reproduction of one made in 1693, rains water down on unsuspecting visitors. A gardener hiding behind a peephole could operate hidden jets in the surrounding rocks upon instructions from the duke.

Sir Thomas Bacon preferred fountains to pools. In his essay, "Of Gardens," he wrote, "For fountains, they are a great beauty and refreshment; but pools mar all, and make the garden unwholesome and full of flies and frogs." He also recommended that fountains be cleaned every day. Basons or pools that contained the fountains were also important decorative features in the Renaissance garden. They were built near the house so they could be looked down upon and also served to reflect light on the house and enliven its facade.

Cascades were constructed in the Renaissance villa gardens, and in the eighteenth and early nineteenth centuries they flourished when the picturesque or natural landscape period of gardening held sway. The aim of that period was to make natural-looking waterfalls, lakes, and rivers and, to achieve that end, streams were dammed up to create large lakes.

The forerunner of the modern swimming pool was the cold bath. Used during the seventeenth and eighteenth centuries for refreshment, these baths were usually situated in a shady place and often fed by a cold spring, so a plunge in one was truly invigorating. Sometimes they were accompanied by a bathhouse and occasionally enclosed.

209

Formal water fountains enjoyed a renewed popularity in the mid-nineteenth century. In 1843 an elaborate fountain supplied by a reservoir nearly three quarters of a mile in circumference was designed and built at Chatsworth by Joseph Paxton, head gardener for the duke of Devonshire. It was named in honor of the Czar Nicholas of Russia in whose honor it was to have first spouted. Unfortunately, the czar never got to Chatsworth, but the fountain still set a world record, in its day, of shooting water 290 feet into the air.

Some of the most beautiful fountains in Victorian London were contained in the Crystal Palace, designed and laid out by Paxton. Fountains were soon mass produced in a wide variety of materials including stone, marble, cast iron, terra-cotta, bronze, lead, and porcelain and were within the reach of the average person. Since that time, fountains have been widely used as ornaments in public parks, gardens, and courtyards.

English ivy frames a wall fountain in which lead sculpture suggests a feeling of coolness against a brick background. *Photo by George Taloumis*

An old molasses barrel, stoutly bound with iron hoops, serves as a miniature pool for water lilies. *Photo by Ronald Rolo*

The sounds that water makes in a wall fountain as it spills from one level to another is a constant source of refreshment. When water is desired as a feature in the garden and space does not allow for a pool, a wall fountain solves the problem. Here brick, cast stone, and cement have been used with taste to create a focal point. English ivy, arborvitae, and water flag (*Iris pseudacorus*), or yellow flag as it is often called, provide harmonious contrasts in form and texture. *Photo by George Taloumis*

An Old World influence pervades this formal pool garden in Santa Barbara, California. Lush tropical foliage softens the light-colored wall with its open-work panels. Two clumps of umbrella plant (*Cyperus alternifolius*) flank the delightful fountain adding to the luxuriance of the entire setting. *Photo by George Taloumis*

For centuries Bacchus, god of revelry, has been a favorite subject for the grotesque masks used in wall fountains to adorn the waterspout and other architectural details related to gardens. They were either cut from stone or molded. *Photo, courtesy Duane Doolittle and Cobb Blake*

Lead cisterns of various sizes, usually elaborately ornamental and once commonly used in European gardens to catch rainwater, rate high as unusual garden ornaments today. Note the bronze bird used as a handle for the water faucet. *Photo by Roche*

A pool as unusual for its design as for its setting is not often seen on a small property. Water lilies, cattail rushes, and weeping willow add materially to the harmonious effect. *Photo by George Taloumis*

Ornamental use of a meandering brook that runs through a garden is made by the addition of a rustic bridge and informal planting. *Photo by J. Horace McFarland Co.*

A pleasant outdoor living area is created alongside a swimming pool by the use of container-grown plants, a living screen for privacy, and simple garden furniture. *Photo, courtesy Brown-Jordan Co.*

A square pool set at an angle to a house of contemporary design creates an interesting and unusual effect. Containers of plants and the use of shrubbery at one side soften the severity of squareness.

This terrace pool made of granite blocks is in complete harmony with its restful, uncluttered surroundings. Here is an example of contemporary landscape design based on low maintenance. *Photos by George Taloumis*

A permanent swimming pool is an asset to the house grounds not only for the pleasure it provides but also for its visual effect. Properly placed, a pool becomes an extension of the garden as well as the house.

A free-form kidney-shaped swimming pool is surrounded by flower beds of informal design.

An attractively landscaped rectangular pool in a small garden. Its ornamental qualities are further enhanced by small sculptured fantail pigeons in the foreground. *Photos by George Taloumis*

A charming small garden makes excellent use of eighteenth century patterns, using boxwood and brick for contrasting texture and color. An unusual brick wall of openwork design is both ornamental and functional; it allows for good air circulation. *Photo, courtesy of Hampfler Photo Studio*

Playfully spurting a stream of water, a fish fountain is the focal point on a brick terrace. Note the unusual form of the circular basin which provides a note of contrast to the parquet brickwork.

Pond lilies serve as natural ornament in a rockobound pool surrounded by native plants.

Pan plays his pipes at the edge of a garden pool surrounded by junipers, boxwood, and other evergreens. *Photos by George Taloumis*

An unusual mosaic design is the focal point of an old lavabo. Mounted on a wall, with a basin below for washing one's hands, lavabos are still occasionally found on garden walls. *Photo by Ronald Rolo*

At the turn of the century and in the years following, garden ornaments like the well shown here, with its tile roof, were commonplace on country estates. Inspiration for design was usually based on Old World models. *Photo by Philip Armsden*

A Verrocchio merchild holding a dolphin makes a charming wall fountain. The graceful design of the iron grille is enhanced by the tuberous begonias set around the basin. *Photo by George Taloumis*

A small secluded garden pool is encircled with flagstone to conceal the concrete construction. The sculptured birdbath speaks for itself. *Photo by Paul E. Genereux*

The natural contours of the land are repeated in the man-made pool which breaks up a large expanse of lawn. Rocks excavated in the areas and placed at the edge of the pool emphasize the makeup of the terrain.

An old stone wellhead is surrounded by formal flower beds and brick walks in the eighteenth century English fashion in one of the restored gardens at Tryon Palace. *Photos by Herbert Rea. Courtesy, Tryon Palace Restoration*

A graceful wall fountain softens the otherwise severe effect of a high brick wall in the Stanly House garden at Tryon Palace, New Bern, North Carolina.

A charming Verrocchio merchild with a dolphin placed in a natural setting would enhance any garden.
Photo by Elizabeth Freeman

15

SUNDIALS

Aɴ Egyptian shadow clock that dates about 1500 ʙ.c. is the earliest known sundial. Obelisks were also used in Egypt and sundials were used by the ancient Greeks and Romans. The reflective dial was an ingenious device, consisting of a small circular mirror affixed to a windowsill or floor. Its purpose was to reflect rays of the sun onto the ceiling which was painted with hour lines and numerals. Sir Isaac Newton is known to have designed a sundial of this type. One of the earliest freestanding sundials is that of column form in the quadrangle of Corpus Christi College, Oxford, dating from 1605.

Gardens before the eighteenth century were laid out in formal geometric patterns and by the end of the sixteenth century, the sundial, mounted on an ornamental pedestal or column, was a popular centerpiece. Clocks were still very expensive as well as scarce, so the sundial was useful as well as ornamental.

The armillary or horological sphere came into favor in the eighteenth century. This ancient astronomical device has roots in pre-Christian times and was probably used for teaching purposes insofar as it is made up of rings representing the important celestial spheres. The armillary sundial has metal rings, one representing the equator, pierced by an arrow, indicating the earth's axis. When well designed and attractively mounted, it is one of the most decorative of all sundials.

Most dials are made of a horizontal plate of metal engraved with numerals, hour lines, and usually a motto, with a projecting arm parallel to the earth's axis. Metals such as brass, copper, or bronze, which do not easily corrode are preferable to cheaper metals such as cast iron. A base or column usually supports the dial; occasionally a sculpted figure is used. Mottoes, usually dwelling on the passage of time, either carved on the dial or on the base, were frequently used; often these inscriptions are in Latin.

The placing of the sundial in the garden is of utmost importance. It must be in the open, away from the shadows cast by buildings or trees. It must also be remembered that sundials, when properly set, give the solar time, not the mean time. Tables can be consulted to work out the difference.

In the sixteenth century, dials were often painted blue with gold hour lines, adding to their ornamental effect in the garden.

Reproductions of old sundials are being made today, as are contemporary designs, and one can be selected to complement almost any garden setting.

222

A sundial of classic design is set on a handsome pedestal enriched with sculptured acanthus leaves. This ornamental piece is located in the garden of the Moffat Ladd House in Portsmouth, New Hampshire. *Photo by Douglas Armsden*

This reproduction of an old dial is called Salem. Its Latin inscription "Time Flies" suggests the eighteenth century practice of using maxims which were inspired by poetic thoughts as contrasted with the foreboding warnings expressed on gravestones.

No matter where this sundial is placed, its reading will prove accurate, provided it is carefully set. Made of bronze, it is mounted on a molded cement pedestal. *Photos, courtesy Leonard V. Short, Jr.*

A reproduction of a nineteenth century sundial on a molded concrete pedestal.

Set on an old millstone, in a late eighteenth century church garden, this dial is a memorial to a man who loved his garden. *Photo by Elizabeth Freeman*

A rock or a boulder or a cut-stone pedestal makes a suitable background for dials of traditional design.

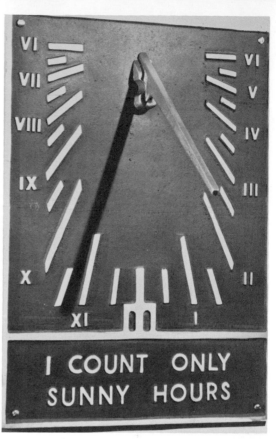

This example is a south vernier sundial, made to be hung on a wall. Its dimensions are 8½″ by 11¾″.

The antique English copper armillary sphere at the Tryon Palace sits on an eighteenth century English carved Purbeck-stone pedestal, surrounded by a low clipped hedge. *Photo by Herbert Rea. Courtesy, Tryon Palace Restoration*

A hand-carved limestone sundial designed to fit in equally well with contemporary or traditional surroundings. *Photos, courtesy Leonard V. Short, Jr.*

226

Surrounded by French hydrangeas and a climbing hydrangea, a gaslight illuminates the entrance to a driveway. *Photo by George Taloumis*

16

COMPLEMENTS AND ACCESSORIES

THE complements and accessories to be found in nearly every garden are so numerous that to feature all of them in pictures would result in a book at least twice the size of this volume. Many of the photographs in these sixteen chapters include not only details and refinements of design that enhance the garden ornaments shown but also a wealth of accessories that lend a finished look to a well-ordered garden. As with the rooms in a house, so with the various units of the home grounds there is the need for lampposts, sections of trellis, ornamental ironwork, a play area for children, a toolhouse, a potting bench, and other necessary features. Many of these items are vital for functional use. Some are strictly utilitarian but all can have eye appeal as well when thought is given to their selection.

The little things in life are often those that give our existence its true meaning. So it is with a garden, large or small. The tools we use, the handle of the faucet, the watering can, the edging for the flower bed, or the garden walk—all contribute to the charm and the beauty of your home grounds and mine. Thus, the sense of order that design implies can be brought to bear in every segment of the property.

Faucets can be decorative as well as functional when bronze knobs are added. Foxes, squirrels, chipmunks, birds of many kinds, butterflies, whales, rabbits, and fish are used as handles to turn the garden faucet. *Photo by Ronald Rolo*

An outdoor area set aside for play is often considered a "must" on the home grounds. Large or small, as space permits, this area need not be an eyesore. Attractively and simply landscaped, with an eye to easy maintenance, play areas are usually screened by a fence or a hedge. A combination of hard and soft surfaces is desirable. Concrete or hot-topped areas provide ample opportunity to ride play vehicles and to roller skate. Grassy plots under swing sets, slides, and other climbing devices help protect the youngsters from injury should they fall.

Play equipment for children is available in many forms. Quality pieces designed for outdoor use come in many colors and are treated to withstand the elements. Well-made swing sets, slides, jungle gyms, and sandboxes should last for many years.

A number of handsome free-form play devices, such as concrete animals and tunnels, are available, not only providing entertainment, but also adding visual enhancement. *Photo by Paul E. Genereux*

Beach stones are both decorative and practical as used in this contemporary planting. The overall effect complements the house.

Another version of the potting bench—enclosed for privacy, convenience, and efficiency. Woodbine offers a decorative touch on the fence.

Fortunate is the gardener with an enclosed area complete with a well-ventilated potting shed and workbench. Such shelters serve as recouping areas for newly potted plants. *Photos by George Taloumis*

Where space permits, a sizable work area, screened from view, is an ideal adjunct to a garden to store containers and potted plants that have finished flowering or to grow material for seasonal flowering. Redwood, used for permanence, has been designed to fit the site.

A neat edging for the flower borders and the peastone path is achieved by the use of brick. *Photo by Paul E. Genereux*

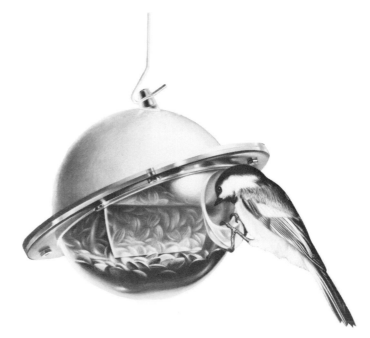

Today the use of mulches is essential to easy garden maintenance and it lends aesthetic appeal as well. Oriental gardeners have used stone in a variety of ways for countless decades and the effects they have achieved have broadened our horizons. Aside from their functional value, stone mulches provide pleasing textural effects, help to define planting areas and accentuate the beauty of plant forms. They need more attention from gardeners as suggested by this approach to an Arizona house. *Photo by George Taloumis*

Opposite: A chickadee feasts on sunflower seeds placed in a Satellite bird feeder. When hung close to the house on a wire stretched between two trees, or on an overhanging roof or a window bracket, this feeder will attract many species of birds, both ground-feeders and clinging types. It is nearly squirrel-proof when hung properly. *Photo, courtesy James R. Waite*

Walls and driveways acquire a trim, finished effect when a permanent edge is provided. Here brick set in concrete has been used to enhance an attractive planting. *Photo by Paul E. Genereux*

A spade, a trowel, a rake, and a watering pot are four basic pieces of every gardener's equipment. All are essential but the watering pot has an ornamental aspect as well. The common galvanized and plastic types usually seen are far less pleasing in design than the hand-hammered copper and tin pots of bygone days. The French copper pots at Mount Vernon never fail to delight visitors. *Photo by Ronald Rolo*

An ancient lilac mulched with crushed stone retained with redwood planks. Heavy rope adds a decorative effect to this low retaining wall.

Tree wells can be made neat in appearance with brick or metal edging. A stone mulch conserves moisture. The wire collar prevents rodent damage to the bark in winter. *Photos by George Taloumis*

Where space permits and gardening enthusiasm is pursued avidly, a toolhouse is a sound investment. Suitable planting of big-scale shrubs makes service buildings inconspicuous.

This utility house used for garden tools, modeled after an eighteenth century "necessary," is conveniently situated near the flower garden. Outbuildings of the period were well designed, usually made of the same material as the main house; hence they were ornamental as well as functional. *Photos by George Taloumis*

A redwood fence makes an effective background for tropical plants along a driveway. A planterlike effect is created by using a tailored edging of redwood to complement the background.

Nineteenth century streetlights are widely reproduced for use in present-day gardens. When they are made with an eye to proper scale and set on sturdy well-designed posts, they are "fittin' to be settin' there." *Photo by Paul E. Genereux*

A nautical-style wall lantern. *Photo, courtesy of Lite Trend*

A guiding light for a harborside home is provided by an antique lantern mounted on a post. *Photos by George Taloumis*

Bibliography

Bacon, Francis. *Of Gardens*. London, 1625.

Berrall, Julia S. *The Garden, An Illustrated History*. New York, 1966.

Bruce, Harold. *The Gardens of Winterthur in All Seasons*. New York, 1968.

Chambers, Sir William. *Designs of Chinese Buildings, Furniture, Dresses, Machines, and Utensils*. London, 1757.

————. *A Dissertation on Oriental Gardening*. London, 1772.

Church, Thomas. *Gardens Are for People*. New York, 1955.

————. *Your Private World, A Study of Intimate Gardens*. San Francisco, 1969.

Clifford, Derek. *A History of Garden Design*. London, 1962.

Coats, Peter. *Great Gardens of Britain*. New York, 1967.

————. *Great Gardens of the Western World*. New York, 1968.

————. *House and Garden Book of Garden Decoration*. New York, 1970.

Crowe, Sylvia. *Garden Design*. New York, 1958.

Dow, George F. *Arts and Crafts in New England*. Topsfield, Mass., 1927.

Downing, Andrew J. *A Treatise on the Theory and Practice of Landscape Gardening*. New York, 1841.

Dutton, Joan Parry. *Enjoying America's Gardens*. New York, 1958.

Dutton, Ralf. *The English Garden*. New York, 1936.

Earle, Alice Morse. *Old Time Gardens*. New York, 1916.

Earnest, Adele. *The Art of the Decoy*. New York, 1965.

Eckbo, Garrett. *Landscape for Living*. New York, 1950.

Edwards, Paul. *English Garden Ornament*. New York, 1965.

Fairbrother, Nan. *Men and Gardens*. New York, 1956.

————. *New Lives, New Landscapes*. New York, 1970.

Faure, Gabriel. *Gardens of Rome*. Fair Lawn, N. J., 1960.

Fitzgerald, Ken. *Weathervanes and Whirligigs*. New York, 1967.

Fletcher, H. L. V. *The Feature Garden*. Newton, Mass., 1961.

Foley, Daniel J. *Gardening by the Sea*. Philadelphia, 1965.

————. *Gardening for Beginners*. New York, 1967.

Fox, Mrs. Helen. *André le Nôtre, Garden Architect to Kings,* 1962.

Fried, Frederick. *Artists in Wood*. New York, 1970.

Gladstone, Bernard. *The Complete Book of Garden and Outdoor Lighting*. New York, 1956.

Gothein, Marie Luise. *A History of Garden Art*. Translated from the German by Mrs. Archer-Hind. London, 1928.

Graham, Dorothy. *Chinese Gardens*. New York, 1938.

Green, David. *Gardener to Queen Anne—Henry Wise*. London, 1956.

Hadfield, Miles. *Gardening in Britain*. Newton, Mass., 1962.

————. *Gardens*. New York, 1962.

Hadfield, Miles and John. *Gardens of Delight*. London, 1964.

Howard, Edwin L.   *Chinese Garden Architecture*. New York, 1931.

Hubbard, H. V. and Kimball, T.   *An Introduction to the Study of Landscape Design*. New York, 1917.

Hussey, Christopher.   *The Picturesque, Studies in a Point of View*. 2d ed. London, 1927.

Hyams, Edward.   *Irish Gardens*. New York, 1967.

Inn, Henry.   *Chinese Houses and Gardens*. New York, 1950.

Ireys, Alice Recknagel.   *How to Plan and Plant Your Own Property*. New York, 1967.

Ishimoto, Tatsuo.   *The Art of the Japanese Garden*. New York, 1958.

Ishimoto, Tatsuo and Kiyoko.   *Japanese Gardens Today*. New York, 1968.

Jackson, Robert, ed.   *Beautiful Gardens of the World*. London, 1953.

Jekyll, Gertrude, and Hussey, Christopher.   *Garden Ornament*. New York, 1927.

Jellicoe, G. A.   *Garden Decoration and Ornament for Smaller Houses*. London, 1936.

Kimball, Fiske.   *Mr. Samuel McIntire, Carver; The Architect of Salem*. Salem, Mass., 1940.

Kincaid, Mrs. Paul.   *Japanese Garden and Floral Art*. New York, 1966.

Kuck, Loraine E.   *The Art of Japanese Gardens*. New York, 1940 and 1969.

Lawson, William.   *New Orchard and Garden*. London, 1618.

Lees, Carlton B.   *Gardens, Plants and Man*. Englewood Cliffs, N.J., 1970.

Leighton, Ann.   *Early American Gardens*. Boston, 1970.

Lemmon, Kenneth.   *The Covered Garden*. London, 1962.

Lockwood, Alice G. B.   *Gardens of Colony and State*. 2 vols. New York, 1931.

Lord, Priscilla Sawyer, and Foley, Daniel J.   *The Folk Arts and Crafts of New England*. Philadelphia, 1965.

Loudon, J. C.   *Encyclopaedia of Cottage, Farm and Villa Architecture and Furniture*. London, 1833.

———. *An Encyclopaedia of Gardening*. London, 1834

———. *The Suburban Gardener and Villa Companion*. London, 1838.

Lynch, Kenneth.   *Garden Ornaments* (General Wholesale Catalogue for the Trade, Number 2066). Wilton, Conn., 1966.

Manwaring, E. W.   *Italian Landscape in Eighteenth Century England*. London, 1925.

Manwaring, Robert.   *The Cabinet and Chair-Maker's Real Friend and Companion*. London, 1765.

Matthews, W. H.   *Mazes and Labyrinths, Their History and Development*. New York, 1970.

Northend, Mary Harrod.   *Garden Ornaments*. New York, 1916.

———. *Memories of Old Salem*. New York, 1917.

Powell, Florence Lee.   *In the Chinese Garden*. New York, 1943.

Repton, Humphrey. *Fragments on the Theory and Practice of Landscape Gardening*. London, 1817.

———. *Observations on the Theory and Practice of Landscape Gardening*. London, 1803.

———. *On the Introduction of Indian Architecture and Gardening*. London, 1808.

———. *Sketches and Hints on Landscape Gardening*. London, 1795.

Robinson, William.   *The English Flower Garden*. London, 1883.

———. *The Wild Garden*. London, 1870.

Rohde, Eleanor Sinclair. *Oxford's College Gardens*. London, 1932.

Schuler, Stanley. *Outdoor Lighting for Your Home*. Princeton, N.J., 1962.

Shaffer, E. T. H. *Carolina Gardens*. New York, 1963.

Shenstone, William. *The Works in Verse and Prose of William Shenstone,* Dodsley's edition. London, 1764–69.

Shepheard, Peter. *Modern Gardens, Masterworks of International Garden Architecture*. New York, 1954.

Shepherd and Jellicoe. *Italian Gardens of the Renaissance*. London, 1925.

Simonds, John O. *Landscape Architecture*. New York, 1961.

Siren, Osvald. *Gardens of China*. New York, 1949.

Snow, Marc. *Modern American Gardens—Designed by James Rose*. New York, 1967.

Steele, Fletcher. *Gardens and People*. Boston, 1964.

Tabor, Grace. *Old-fashioned Gardening*. New York, 1913.

Taloumis, George. *Outdoor Gardening in Pots and Boxes*. New York, 1962.

Thomas, Dr. G. L., Jr. *Garden Pools, Water-Lilies and Goldfish*. Princeton, N.J., 1958.

Thomas, Gertrude Z. *Richer Than Spices*. New York, 1965.

Thomas, Sir William Beach. *Gardens*. London, 1952.

Tunnard, Christopher. *Gardens in the Modern Landscape*. 2d ed. London, 1948.

Vaux, Calvert. *Villas and Cottages*. New York, 1870.

White, J. E. Grant. *Garden Art and Architecture*. New York, 1968.

Whitehill, Walter Muir. *George Crowninshield's Yacht, Cleopatra's Barge, and a Catalogue of the Francis B. Crowninshield Gallery*. Salem, Mass., 1959.

Whittle, Tyler. *Some Ancient Gentlemen*. New York, 1966.

Williams, C. A. S. *Encylopedia of Chinese Symbolism and Art Motives*. New York, 1960.

Wilson, Ernest Henry. *China, Mother of Gardens*. Boston, 1929.

Sources for Garden Ornaments and Accessories

MANY manufacturers of garden ornaments and accessories advertise in the leading home and garden magazines. Catalogues, brochures, and descriptive circulars may be obtained from most of these firms upon request or for a small fee.

Antique Shops. Those known for the quality of their collections are prime sources for unusual pieces of sculpture and a wide variety of garden ornaments as well.

Arts and Crafts Societies. With the revival of interest in all types of handcrafts, an ever-growing number of societies are focusing attention on exhibitions and sales featuring ceramics, metalwork, and sculpture including garden ornaments.

Auctions. Leading auction houses throughout the country frequently dispose of unusual garden ornaments. Occasionally, a notable collection of more than casual interest is placed on the market.

Community Dumps. Many a treasure has been found on the town dump.

Flower Shops. The well-established flower shop often proves to be an excellent source of imported garden ornaments as well as those produced locally.

Garden Centers. Many garden centers which specialize primarily in plant material, garden gadgets, and lawn supplies offer a wide selection of garden ornaments of varying quality.

Junk Dealers, Wrecking Companies, and Used Furniture Shops. The search for exceptional pieces—architectural and sculptural, fountains, iron gates, sections of fences, posts, finials, and containers of various kinds—may often be pursued with surprising success from these sources. Usually prices are moderate.

Museums. Many of our leading museums offer reproductions of sculpture, ship figureheads, sternboard carvings, and the like in gift shops under museum sponsorship. A number of small museums periodically sponsor exhibits by sculptors and master craftsmen in the field of ceramics and metal. Frequently, unusual pieces can be purchased.

Oriental Shops, Gift and Specialty Shops. Dealers in reproductions of lanterns, containers of classical design, sculpture, and other garden ornaments are far more numerous than is generally realized.

GARDEN ORNAMENTS ACCESSORIES (GENERAL):

Harriet Carter
Plymouth Meeting, Pennsylvania 19462

J. F. Day & Company
2820 6th Avenue S.
Birmingham, Alabama 35233

Jorge Epstein
(Antique Garden Materials)
487 Norfolk Street
Mattapan, Massachusetts 02126

Florentine Craftsmen
650–654 First Avenue (37th St.)
New York, New York 10016

Kenneth Lynch & Sons, Inc.
Wilton, Connecticut 06897

Moultrie Manufacturing Company
Moultrie, Georgia 31768

Patio City—J. J. Kilbel
4669 Akron-Cleveland Road
Peninsula, Ohio 44264

Postamatic Company
Box 160
Lafayette Hill, Pennsylvania 19444

The Ragged Sailor
Camden, Maine 04843 and
Tiburon, California 94920

Tuscany Studio
163 W. Ohio Street
Chicago, Illinois 60610

BIRDBATHS:

Florentine Craftsmen
650–654 First Avenue (37th St.)
New York, New York 10016

Kenneth Lynch & Sons, Inc.
Wilton, Connecticut 06897

The Ragged Sailor
Camden, Maine 04843 and
Tiburon, California

Tuscany Studio
163 W. Ohio Street
Chicago, Illinois 60610

BIRD FEEDERS:

Local Audubon Societies

Hummingbird Heaven
6818-H Apperson Street
Tujunga, California 91042

The Mill House
Box 13265
Station E
Oakland, California

James R. Waite
Box 78–HJ1
Manhasset, New York 11030

Woodsworld
600E Olive Springs Road
East Santa Cruz, California 95060

FENCES AND SHELTERS:

California Redwood Association
617 Montgomery Street
San Francisco, California 90411

Walpole Woodworkers, Inc.
Dept. 701
764 East Street
Walpole, Massachusetts 02081

GARDEN FURNITURE:

When a specific type of furniture is desired, manufacturers such as these listed will supply names of local dealers.

Ames Aire Furniture Company
Parkersburg, West Virginia 26101

Atlanta Stove Works, Inc.
P.O. Box 5254
Atlanta, Georgia 30307

Basket House
89 W. Main Street
Rockaway, New Jersey 07866

Birmingham Ornamental Iron Company
Box 1911
Birmingham, Alabama 35201

Brown-Jordan Company
Box 1269
9860 Gidley
El Monte, California 91734

Ficks Reed Company
4900 Charlemar Drive
Cincinnati, Ohio 45227

The Lakeside House
P.O. Box 486
White Rock, South Carolina 29177

Molla Furniture
Molla, Inc.
D & D Building
979 Third Avenue
New York, New York 10022

Moultrie Manufacturing Company
Moultrie, Georgia 31768

The Patio
P.O. Box 2843
San Francisco, California 94126

Scroll, Inc.
800 N.W. 166th Street
Miami, Florida 33164

Siesta Manufacturing Company, Inc.
P.O. Box 574
Sarasota, Florida 33578

Tropi-Cal
5731 S. Alameda Street
Los Angeles, California

Tropitone Furniture Company, Inc.
Sarasota, Florida 33578

Willow & Reed
315 East 62nd Street
New York, New York 10021

POOLS AND FOUNTAINS:

Astra Company
Box 4351
St. Louis, Missouri 63123

Bello-Groppi Studio
421 W. Wisconsin Avenue
Chicago, Illinois 60614

The Fountainhead Studios
Essex, Massachusetts 01929

Hermitage Gardens
W. Seneca Avenue
Canastota, New York 13032

Michigan Bulb Company
Grand Rapids, Michigan 49502

Old South Forge Division
Moultrie, Georgia 31768

Pacific Palm Pools
P.O. Box 147
615 Loudonville Road
Latham, New York 12110

Paradise Gardens
Route 18
Whitman, Massachusetts 02382

Rain Jet Corporation
301 South Flower Street
Burbank, California 91503

Tuscany Studio
163 W. Ohio St.
Chicago, Illinois 60610

EXTERIOR DECORATIVE HARDWARE:

J. C. De Jong & Company, Inc.
Jamaica, New York 11433

Moultrie Manufacturing Company
Moultrie, Georgia 31768

OUTDOOR LIGHTING:

Gordon A. Brewer
Village Coppersmith
100 Third Street South
St. Petersburg, Florida

Carr Lighting Company
P.O. Box 3894 T. A.
Los Angeles, California 90054

Georgian Art Lighting Design, Inc.
P.O. Box 325
Lawrenceville, Georgia 30245

Hadco Products
P.O. Box 128
Littlestown, Pennsylvania 17340

The Lamp Crafters
Box 501
Lawrenceville, Georgia 30245

Ruby Lighting Corp.
Department 1
128 Fifth Avenue
New York, New York 10011

PLANTERS AND CONTAINERS:

Architectural Pottery
2020 S. Robertson
Los Angeles, California 90034

Walt Nicke
Box 71H
Hudson, New York 12534

The Ragged Sailor
Camden, Maine 04843 and
Tiburon, California 94920

Scargo Stoneware Pottery
Box 304
Route 6A
Dennis, Massachusetts 02638

Many professional potters can be found in local communities.

RAILROAD TIES AND
   REDWOOD PLANKS:

A & K Railroad Materials, Inc.
3438 Helen Street
Oakland, California 94608

SCULPTURE:

Bello-Groppi Studio
421 W. Wisconsin Avenue
Chicago, Illinois 60614

Florentine Craftsmen
650–654 First Avenue (37th St.)
New York, New York 10016

John Frongelo
Fountainhead Studios
Essex, Massachusetts 01929

Hartwell Kennard
1015-H Nyssa Street
McAllen, Texas 78501

M. Knoedler & Company
21 E. 70th Street
New York, New York 10021

Kenneth Lynch & Sons, Inc.
Wilton, Connecticut 06897

The Ragged Sailor
Camden, Maine 04843 and
Tiburon, California 94920

The Sculpture Center
167 E. 69th Street
New York, New York 10021

Sculpture Collectors
185 Madison Avenue
New York, New York 10016

SUNDIALS:

Florentine Craftsmen
650–654 First Avenue (37th St.)
New York, New York 10016

Kenneth Lynch & Sons, Inc.
Wilton, Connecticut 06897

Sun Dials
Box #3
New Ipswich, New Hampshire 03071

WALL ORNAMENTS:

Arborlite, Inc.
East Brookfield, Massachusetts 01515

John R. Burbidge
12 Stafford Road
Danvers, Massachusetts 01923

Louis Mangifesti
Haverhill Street
Reading, Massachusetts 01867

WEATHER VANES:

J. W. Fiske, Inc.
111 Pennsylvania Avenue
Paterson, New Jersey 07500

Kenneth Lynch & Sons, Inc.
Wilton, Connecticut 06897

E. G. Washburne & Company, Inc.
85 Andover Street
Danvers, Massachusetts 01923

R. Watkins
P.O. Box 142
Deer Park, New York 11729

Whitehall Metal Studios, Inc.
Montague, Michigan 49437

WESTERN WAGON WHEELS:

Springer Manufacturing Company
Box 17083
Portland, Oregon 92717

Index